GROWING
UP
THIN

GROWING UP THIN

□

Alvin N. Eden, M.D.

with Joan Rattner Heilman

□

David McKay Company, Inc.

NEW YORK

To my family

Library of Congress Cataloging in Publication Data

Eden, Alvin N.
  Growing up thin.

  Includes index.
  1. Children—Nutrition. 2. Children—Growth.
3. Leanness. I. Heilman, Joan Rattner, joint author.
II. Title.
RJ206.E33   613.2'5'024054   75-8905
ISBN 0-679-50543-1

Preface

This book is dedicated to you, the parents and future parents of all our children. It is written by an angry and frustrated pediatrician who has been watching children become fatter and fatter, growing up into fat unhealthy adults, while we all stand helplessly by. I want to do something about it and I think I can. I am convinced that my methods can help eradicate obesity, the number-one public health problem in the United States today.

Let me teach you how to "fatproof" your baby. Let me show you how to thin down your youngster. Let me help you raise a thin, healthy child.

Contents

List of Tables

NOTE: Because we believe in equality of the sexes, and because the English language provides no graceful words to substitute for "his" and "her" and "he" and "she," we have decided to alternate the genders and give equal time chapter to chapter. In all cases, naturally, we are referring to both girls and boys. We start off with a "he," a decision made by the flip of a coin.

Foreword

There is some similarity between obesity and the weather in that obesity is also a subject frequently "talked about but nothing done about." It is well established that overweight individuals are not as healthy, comfortable, happy, nor long-lived as people of normal weight. The overweight individual is discriminated against in employment, in education, and probably in mate selection. In many ways, life is quite unfair to him.

When one is obese, the most frequent remark heard (often made "behind one's back") is, "How did he let himself get that way?" or, "Why did he wait so long to reduce?" All too often the question *should* be, "Couldn't his parents have prevented his overweight?" As dramatic as cures are, prevention must be more dramatic. The soundest, most effective "cure" of obesity is its *prevention,* and this prevention belongs in childhood—before the agonies of obesity have time to set in.

Obesity need not be the same as the weather. Something can be done about it—before it really develops. Dr. Alvin N. Eden has written a book that ably presents this thesis. His ideas are sound and scientific, readable and understandable. The book fills a void, both for the parent and the professional. It is time for a good book addressed to a real need of the younger generation. I'm glad it was written. You will be also.

MORTON B. GLENN, M.D.

1

Fatproofing Your Child

This is *not* another diet book. I am not going to give you a miracle diet for fat, because there is no such thing, though I certainly am going to suggest what your child should and shouldn't eat. I am going to show you how to bring up a thin, healthy child who will have little chance of becoming a fat adult.

The best answer to fat is to prevent it before it begins—or to short-circuit it before it's too late. It can be done and it's easy. I know my approach works because it has been successful in treating many hundreds of children I have seen in my own practice.

I call it "fatproofing" your child. Just as fireproofing your house will prevent it from burning down, fatproofing your child will prevent him from becoming a hopelessly fat adult. The earlier you start fatproofing, preferably even before birth, the better it will work because it's difficult to raise a very fat baby to be a thin adolescent. A child can become thin at any age, but it gets harder to accomplish with each passing year. And the longer he is fat, the greater his chances of staying that way.

Babies Learn Fast

Very early in his life, a baby learns what and how much to eat. His eating patterns are formed in his first six months or a year; they are reinforced and almost solidified by the time he is two. By six or seven, his likes and dislikes, appetite and capacity may be set for life unless a determined effort is made to modify them.

Research has shown that for many people overweight is predetermined by their experiences in early childhood. Perhaps 90 percent of the extremely obese adults were started on that path when they were babies. The reasons: possibly a genetic tendency towards overweight—fat does tend to run in families; a superabundance of fat cells which people who have been fat since childhood possess, and which, for some still-unknown reason, helps them cling to fat; the development of the habit of eating too much; a pattern of eating the wrong foods; plus a predisposition or learned habit of physical inactivity.

A baby may begin to grow fat before birth if he is born to a markedly overweight mother who not only overfeeds herself but the baby as well. *That is why prospective mothers who are heavy would be wise to lose weight before they become pregnant.*

Who Will Probably Grow Up Fat, Unhealthy, Unhappy?

- an infant who is overstuffed with milk, who has a bottle stuck into his mouth whenever he frets, hungry or not
- the baby who is fed solid foods much too early, and

is pressured to consume more and more by a mother who is afraid the baby will starve to death before supper

• the toddler who is incarcerated in a playpen or a stroller or who is bribed with goodies to finish his lunch

• the preschooler who is encouraged to watch TV in order to give his mother some peace and quiet, and who whines for candy and cookies and gets them

• the school-age child who is driven to and from school and eats junk food without stop when he's home and fills up at the corner store in between

• the adolescent who actually becomes malnourished because he seldom eats with the family, consumes low-nutrition, high-calorie food straight out of the vending machine or quick-food store, instead of fruit and vegetables and milk, who never walks when he can sit and never runs when he can walk

My Suggestions for Raising Thin, Healthy Children

If, on the other hand, you follow my step-by-step plan for raising thin and healthy children, you will:

• slim down before you become pregnant

• feed your baby only as much as he needs in order to grow and gain weight at a normal rate (as determined by your pediatrician)

• offer well-balanced nutritious food with a minimum of "junk foods"

• serve three regular meals a day, never substituting snacks for meals

• fatproof your house by getting rid of all the high-calorie low-nutrition foods. Keep a supply of healthy snacks on hand

• eliminate the bribes and rewards for eating

• feed everyone in the family the same way

- create a positive environment for exercise
- cut out the nagging and overinvolvement with every mouthful, the pressuring and struggling to get your child to eat—or *not* eat

AND

- stop feeling guilty for doing *right* by your child. Stick to your guns and your healthy habits and remember that parents who truly love their children *do not* demonstrate their love by overfeeding them

Fat Now, Fat Later

A thin child almost always grows up to be a thin adult.

A fat child almost always grows up to be a fat adult.

Only now are people beginning to realize that it is not good to raise a fat child. When those of us who are adults were children, our parents *knew* they must stuff us full of food, that a clean plate was the best. To show their love for us, they fed us and made us plump. If they weren't successful, they worried and fretted and pushed and pressured—"Finish your dinner. The children in Europe are starving."

Though scientific research has clearly shown that it's often impossible for a fat baby to turn into a thin adult, a fat baby is still what many parents strive for. I know, because I fight this attitude every day in my practice as a pediatrician.

Equating fatness with good health is part of our culture. It undoubtedly originated back in the time when a great many children were underfed and suffering from malnutrition. In those days, a thin baby may actually have been starving and therefore was definitely not in good health. The nice plump baby was obviously not deprived of good food and so was considered healthy.

Today, in this affluent country, children—except, of

course, those who live in poverty—are well fed. The problem, in fact, has become just the opposite of starvation. More and more babies and children are *overfed* and overweight as well. American children have been shown to be 10 percent taller in this century than they were earlier—but 20 to 30 percent heavier.

I have been a pediatrician for twenty years, and my main function is the treatment and prevention of disease in infants, children and adolescents. While many diseases can now be prevented by immunization and others treated by medication, next to the old-fashioned cold the commonest disease for which there is not yet a specific cure is *fat*. Once it's there for any length of time, it has a tenacious tendency to remain for life.

As a pediatrician, therefore, I would not be doing my job if I didn't attempt to immunize my patients against it or to get rid of it in time to prevent an unhappy future.

Some Statistics

Eighty-five percent of fat children grow up to fight fat all their lives. Along the way, they are going to find the going rough as they try to survive in a thin world that considers fat to be ugly as well as immoral.

Estimates put the number of overweight Americans anywhere from 25 to 45 percent, with overweight children at 30 percent, some of them merely a few pounds out of line and others definitely obese (weighing over 20 percent more than they should).

The diet industry in this country is tremendous, with "new" methods of weight reduction constantly appearing on the scene. Low-calorie foods and artificial sweeteners have become a $700,000,000-a-year industry. Billions of dollars are spent annually to help fat Americans lose weight, unfortunately with a high relapse rate. The only solution to the problem is to start with the children, to keep them thin from the beginning so that they'll have a good chance of remaining thin the rest of their lives.

Once a person has become an obese adult, it is extremely difficult ever to shed weight. According to Dr. C. S. Chlouverakis, director of the Obesity and Lipid Abnormalities Service at the E. J. Meyer Memorial Hospital in Buffalo, N.Y., "Only 25 percent of grossly overweight persons are able to lose as much as twenty-five pounds and 5 percent forty pounds. Routine treatment of one hundred consecutive obese patients in the obesity clinic of a large teaching hospital was even less successful; only 12 percent were able to lose twenty pounds and only one patient lost forty pounds. Two years after the end of treatment only two patients had maintained the weight loss."

Fat and Happy?

While fat children may be considered adorable, fat adults are not. While fat children are usually thought to be superhealthy (though they're not), fat adults have been proved to be susceptible to debilitating ailments, accidents, and early deaths. While everyone loves a fat baby, hardly anyone loves a fat adolescent or adult. They are discriminated against by peers, employers, college admissions officers, the opposite sex, even their own families. Even fat young children beyond their earliest years are scorned and rejected because they are "different."

Fat people, children included, are seldom jolly. They're usually unhappy and depressed, emotionally traumatized every day of their lives.

Our Fat Society

Nevertheless, our society is growing fatter earlier. In my practice, I see increasing numbers of fat children coming through my door. So does every other pediatrician in the country. Obesity, a dangerous, insidious and treacherous disease, has become, according to Senator Edward M. Kennedy, who spoke recently before the Senate Select Committee on Nutrition and Human Needs, "America's number-one health defect. While children of West Africa melt away from starvation, America stands in ironic contrast as a land of the overindulged and excessively fed. In many ways, the well-being of the overfed is as threatened as that of the undernourished."

As we become more affluent and less physically active, we are eating too much food for our energy needs. If you add to that the fact that we consume huge amounts of non-nutritious calorie-laden foods rather than the recommended well-balanced diet, you'll see that our children are in great danger of becoming a generation of unhealthy, unhappy, fat-fighting people who will always be on a diet.

Where once we ate only the necessary amount to keep our bodies functioning (or were actually undernourished) and toiled hard enough to burn it off, today we merely expand. The typical American child is started on baby foods at much too young an age, learns to fill up on sodas and cookies and candy, is driven door to door in an automobile, has few if any chores to do, and spends many hours a day watching television commercials that urge him to demand that his mother buy unhealthy foods.

While Americans have set the pace, other nations that have become affluent, urbanized and mechanized are following our example. Studies have shown, for instance, that the Japanese are growing fatter, as they are becoming richer and more sedentary.

The Alaskan Eskimos, now in the midst of an economic boom, have developed a new "disease," recently described at an obesity symposium by Dr. David Coursin. After many months of eating a Western-style, high-calorie, sugar- and starch-rich diet, the time comes when they find they can't get their parkas closed any more, a difficulty that Dr. Coursin calls the "parka syndrome." Even the Bantu tribe of Africa has grown in girth as its members have moved from poor rural areas to the richer cities.

Who's in Charge Around Here?

Parents are the only ones who can reverse the trend, and I want to convince at least a few parents to remember that's just who you are—the people in charge around here. And that you must make the major household decisions, such as what food is served in your homes.

I am a pediatrician and I speak to parents all day long. And I can tell you that I am constantly dismayed when I see that children barely out of diapers are giving orders to their elders. I'm dismayed to see the results—more and more overweight children, little people who are fat because their parents have taken the line of least resistance, have copped out, and are feeding them the wrong foods because that's "what the children want."

I am tired of parents being frightened of their children. I am tired of watching them make excuses for raising a fat child who will not thank them for it later. I am tired of parents who are terrified of losing their children's love.

These little children are going to become big children and then big adults, who will always eat in an unhealthy way because their parents are afraid to "deprive" them of everything they demand.

Parents, Take Charge

It's time for parents to assume their responsibilities. They are the members of the family who should guide and mold, who have more experience and certainly better judgment than a little child, a medium-sized child, and even an adolescent. Just as children shouldn't have the responsibility of choosing a house to live in, or picking out the car to buy, or the new job their father should take, neither should they decide what food comes into the house.

Certainly they can make requests. Certainly they don't have to eat everything you present to them. But certainly, too, there is no need for you to feel guilty when you say "no" to a bag of sugar-coated whosies or "not now" to a package of munchies. Or, "We don't drink that," to a bottle of imitation grape soda. It is your job as parents to decide what is eaten in your home.

Children do not really want to be in charge of their worlds. Though they may push and pressure and demand, they want boundaries and direction. And though they'll assume the leadership position if it's given to them, it frightens and worries them to have it. The permissiveness that has permeated our society has not made children happier, nor has it made them feel more loved.

Is It Real Love?

Producing a fat, undisciplined child is not a demonstration of real love. Rather, it is misguided love that leads a mother to overstuff her baby or to allow her child to eat too much of the wrong foods and spend too many hours on his backside in front of the television set—just as it's misguided love to let him jump off a roof because he feels like it. Children have to be shown what is acceptable and not acceptable. And it is not acceptable to get fat and lazy.

We don't need to feel the least bit guilty when we "deprive" our children of the wrong kinds of food, because we are depriving them only of an unhappy childhood and a miserable and perhaps unhealthy adulthood. The stakes are high, but a child cannot be expected to know that excess fat means something has gone wrong.

The goal of parents is to raise a healthy, happy, well-adjusted child. You are not accomplishing that goal if you raise a fat child.

Give Him the "Eyeball Test"

How do you know if your child is too fat? The best method of determining that is to *look* at him. Nutritionists call this the "eyeball test." If he has rolls around his middle, an extra chin, lumpy legs, he is fat.

But, because many parents do not look at their children objectively (some mothers, for example, are so weight-conscious that they consider anything but a skinny child to be fat; while others, usually fat themselves, would not categorize their youngsters as overweight unless they are grossly so), it is best to consult a pediatrician. Though many doctors are not yet adequately involved with the problems of obesity, they are still in the best position to give counsel.

Being overweight according to the much-used height-weight charts doesn't necessarily mean a child is fat. The body is composed of two main components—the "lean body mass" which is primarily bone, muscle and water, plus the adipose, or fat, tissue. An obese child's body contains too much fat tissue in proportion to his lean body mass, and this can be measured by skin-fold tests and other scientific methods if they seem necessary.

Some children, who weigh more than the charts indicate, have heavy bones or muscular builds. A football player, for example, may weigh 220 pounds and not be fat because he is "all muscle."

In truth, there is no precisely ideal weight for a child at any given moment, but rather a range of possible normal weights. That is why the doctor's "eyeball test" probably gives the best answer.

There *is* a way to fatproof your children. There is a method and it works. Not only that, but it is safe, painless and guaranteed. This is what this book is all about. I am going to take you through childhood, a stage at a time, and show you how to fight fat from infancy right through adolescence.

If your youngster has already become fat, I will show you how to thin him down. Not by putting him on a strict diet, because the usual diets don't work. They leave the child hungry, are too complicated for him (and his mother) to cope with day after day. Besides, in most households, diets lead to arguments, rejection and more misery.

Watch Out for Fad Diets

The fad diets that promise to take off many pounds in a hurry are *dangerous* for children. They often do not provide adequate nutrition for youngsters who are still growing, and they may cause a negative nitrogen balance causing the body to use up needed protein which could curtail full normal growth.

In addition, most of the quick diets take off weight in the

form of water, not fat tissue. Once a person begins to eat normally again, the water accumulates once more. Anyway, few people, especially children, can stay on a strange diet for very long.

If you read straight through this book, you will see that I have frequently repeated some essential information. This is because some of you may skip ahead to the chapters applying specifically to your own child and so miss some important information.

There will probably be an added bonus for you in this book: if you are overweight yourselves, a side effect may be that you'll slim down too. Because my method is a family affair, that's just what has happened with the parents of many of my small patients.

Forget the Pills

Appetite suppressants, injections, and hormones like thyroid (except in very, very rare cases to be determined only by very careful tests) are *dangerous* and contraindicated in children. Besides, they don't work.

2

The Hazards of Fat

What's so bad about being fat? Why am I, a pediatrician, concerned about fatness in children?

What's bad about being fat is that it is dangerously unhealthy. It shortens the life span. It leads to a much higher than normal incidence of very serious disorders, including coronary heart disease, high blood pressure, kidney and circulatory disorders, hernia, arthritis, diabetes, gallstones, and more.

Being fat makes people more likely to have accidents, both fatal and non-fatal.

Fat promotes a sedentary, inactive life-style, another route leading directly toward early death from heart attacks.

Fat makes people miserable because, not only do they feel and look unattractive, but they are discriminated against and persecuted in countless ways by a society that considers fat to be ugly.

Physical Health

There's an extremely high correlation between obesity and the incidence of medical problems. Children who are markedly overweight suffer more consistently from respiratory illnesses than thin children. Adults who are fat, especially those who have always been too heavy, will probably die earlier than they should and suffer assorted unnecessary debilitating diseases.

The Heart Association, for example, lists eight factors that make a person a high risk for strokes and heart attacks. They include high blood pressure, increased blood fats (cholesterol), lack of regular exercise, cigarette smoking, stress, family history and *obesity*. Just being appreciably overweight is considered a risk factor all by itself because of the huge load and strain it places on the cardiovascular system.

Obesity can lead to high blood pressure, another risk factor, with the prevalence correlating neatly with the amount of excess weight a person carries around. Elevated blood pressure is usually caused by atherosclerosis, a plugging up of the blood vessels by fatty deposits, to which obese people are more susceptible. This is because of a high level of cholesterol and triglycerides found in their blood, often because of faulty eating habits.

Overweight people, because they find it harder to get around, don't get enough exercise, another factor. Because they don't build up strong heart muscle and they fail to develop the collateral circulation of blood to the heart, the danger of early sudden death moves closer.

In 1972, 752,000 Americans died of heart disease, making it our leading cause of death. Statistically, one in five of my small patients will have heart disease before he is sixty. This is a frightening thought.

There are now over four million known diabetics in this country, with many more potential candidates. The fact is that "in 85 percent of all adult diabetics," according to the U.S. Public Health Service, "obesity preceded the onset of the disease."

people, with their built-in prejudice against fat, equate heavy people with lack of self-discipline and ability. One employment agency reported that the company had received thousands of requests from potential employers for "thin" people, and only one in twenty-five years for a "plump" one—and that from a manufacturer of clothes for overweight men.

The agency also made a survey of 15,000 executives chosen at random from their clients in fifteen cities. Results showed that the average fat executive receives less pay than a lean one, and that he is less likely to advance as quickly or as high. Only 9 percent of top executives were more than ten pounds overweight; while nearly 40 percent of lower-level executives weighed too much.

Even the U.S. Army refuses overweight applicants and insists that its soldiers maintain "desirable weight levels." The U.S. Navy does the same and will recommend an excessively heavy member of the force for discharge "due to unsuitability."

It obviously does not pay to be overweight. The hazards are real and devastating and no child should be forced to face them by growing up fat.

3

The Causes of Fat

A child may be overweight for a number of different reasons, or, more likely, a combination of reasons. Let's take up these multiple causes one at a time.

Could It Be Genes?

It's been known for many years that fat runs in families, with studies demonstrating that 50 *percent* of the children born of one obese parent and 80 *percent* of those born of two obese parents become fat themselves. Conversely, only 10 percent of the children of thin parents grow up with a weight problem. Does this mean that some children are doomed to be fat? That fat is inherited like blue eyes, curly hair and big noses?

The truth seems to be that some children *are* inherently predisposed to overweight and so will probably always have to be on the alert. The truth also is that overeating and underexercising will complete the job. People with a predisposition to overweight, as well as many of those without it, will *get* fat from eating more than their bodies burn up in activity. As Dr. Jean Mayer puts it, "We—all living creatures—are the result of the interaction of our genetic determinants *and* the environment." In other words, some people have a genetic tendency to become heavy; if they eat too much of the wrong foods and exercise too little, they will get fat more easily than other people.

Research has shown that there is definitely a genetic component to obesity. The best evidence comes from research done many years ago on a group of adopted children. It was found that if two obese people adopt a child born of thin natural parents, the child's chances of becoming excessively fat are much smaller than they would be if she were a natural child born to obese parents.

I remember a couple, both in the 300-pound range, who brought their six-month-old baby to my office as a new patient. I was told he had been born at seven pounds, and I found he now weighed sixteen pounds which was in perfect proportion to his height. I was pleased, assuming that the parents were so concerned with weight that they were careful not to overfeed him.

However, what I didn't know at the time was that the baby had been adopted and had had thin natural parents. Not being faced with the genetic aspect of obesity, he had a much better chance not to end up fat.

In a much more limited study made of identical twins, who, for various reasons, were separated since early child-hood and brought up in different households, it was found that as adults each set of twins ended up very close in weight, as well as height.

A classic piece of research by H. H. Newman and others in 1937 reported in a book entitled *Twins: A Study of Heredity and Environment* compared the average differences in body weight of identical twins (who always have identical genetic characteristics) to fraternal twins and non-twins (who do not). As adults, only 2 percent of the identical twins differed by more than twelve pounds, as opposed to over 50 percent of the fraternal twins and non-twins.

What Is Inherited?

Exactly what produces the tendency to be thin or fat is still conjecture. Experts have made educated guesses but we do not know for sure what the answers are.

One theory is that the regulatory center for appetite, located in the part of the brain called the hypothalamus, may be genetically set higher or lower in different people. Named the "appestat" by Dr. Norman Joliffe, the famed nutritionist, this appetite-regulation setting could be inherited.

Another theory, according to the National Institutes of Health, is that some newborns are inherently susceptible to excess production of insulin and HGH (human growth hormone) which, triggered by overnutrition, may encourage excess fat storage in the body. In other words, an overfed infant may overproduce these hormones which will stimulate the deposition of fat in the tissues.

Too, the genes may determine the way in which a person absorbs, digests and excretes food.

Or, abnormally high numbers of fat cells may be inherited.

Body build, passed down from parent to child, is another important factor in determining whether a child will be fat or thin or in between. A relatively small group of the population, for example, are "ectomorphs," people who have relatively small bodies and long legs and arms with long tapered fingers. These people usually have small appetites, but no matter how much they eat they are not likely to have a weight problem.

On the other hand, "mesomorphs," who are sturdy and

muscular, and particularly the "endomorphs," who tend to be shorter, rounder and softer, with shorter arms and legs, often have considerable difficulty in maintaining normal weight. Because their bodies tend to accrue fat more easily, they must work against it more strenuously. In addition, not only total body build, but the proportions of certain areas of the body run in families, such as buttocks, legs and breasts.

Says Dr. Jules Hirsch, senior physician at Rockefeller University and an important researcher in the field of childhood obesity, "Given the right feeding circumstances, some children can become fat and some cannot. The ectomorphic infant is relatively protected against obesity. But in our society, given the glut of foods and constant barrage of eating stimuli, a certain percentage of endormorphs and mesomorphs become obese."

But Fat Isn't Necessary

My feeling is that while inherited tendencies to be over-weight are certainly of great importance, we should use them as early warning signals. In other words, even a confirmed endomorph, round and soft, with a hearty appetite and two fat parents, and maybe a fat grandmother thrown in, needn't be fat herself. If that child's parents are aware of her inheritance right from the start, even *before* she is born, if they concentrate earlier and harder on the problem, she'll have a fighting chance of growing up thin and healthy.

Once they realize that their child is susceptible to fat, that she gains weight much too easily, then they can take a firm stand against it by not overfeeding and underexercising her.

When I see newborns in the hospital or new patients in my office, part of my routine is to find out what the family's weight pattern is. Sometimes it's not easy. For example, I remember a mother who came looking perfectly normal in weight, with a tremendously fat eighteen-month-old child, a new patient. The baby was already more than ten pounds overweight, with big rolls of fat that made it hard for him to toddle along. His mother wanted to know what to do about the rash on his inner thighs caused by the constant friction.

The baby checked out to be quite healthy and active, and I turned to the subject of his weight. I discovered that, while the father was long and lanky, the mother had been quite obese and had recently shed 105 pounds. Most surprising to me, she didn't seem at all concerned about the baby's size.

After a long discussion about the problems of the obesity already created for the child and those he would encounter if he was allowed to remain fat, his mother agreed to cooperate with me in slimming him down. We diluted the milk, his between-meal snacks changed from cookies and ice cream to fruit, and he was allowed to get a lot more exercise. Now, two years later, he is only three or four pounds over an ideal weight.

Too Many Fat Cells

We can't do a thing about our children's genes. But children with genes tipped toward fat can grow up thin, while those without a family history of overweight can grow up fat, depending on what we do starting at the very beginning of their lives.

We know this because of a startling discovery made only a few years ago by researchers, primarily Dr. Jules Hirsch and Dr. Jerome L. Knittle, at the Rockefeller University in New York. Drs. Hirsch and Knittle did their first work on rats, dividing twenty-six newborn rats into two groups, each with a normal nursing mother. The first group of newborns numbered only four and these grew fat. The second group numbered twenty-two and these, because so many had to compete for food from only one mother, grew up lean.

After weaning, all the young rats were offered a normal rat diet. The lean rats (the deprived group) stayed thin, while the fat rats (the affluent group) remained fat.

Through tests which counted and weighed their fat cells, it was concluded that the rats that grew fat soon after birth had developed an abnormally large number of fat cells which they never shed.

Back in 1962, another group of investigators headed by S. C. Peckham of the U.S. Naval Hospital in San Diego, California, reported that obese animals had a larger number of fat cells in their bodies than thin animals, and that once they'd been fat and then reduced, it was always easier for them to become fat again.

Drs. Knittle and Ginsberg extended the research to people at Mount Sinai Medical Center in New York and discovered that people who have been fat ever since childhood have an abnormally high number of fat-storage, or adipose, cells in their bodies, and that the *earlier* in life obesity begins, the *greater* the number of these cells.

According to their findings, stated simply, an overfed and therefore fat child will develop tremendous numbers of fat cells, many more than a normally thin youngster. These cells will stay with her permanently, despite the most stringent diets.

The two doctors studied 200 children between the ages of two and sixteen and found that a fat two-year-old already has a significantly greater number of these cells than a thin two-year-old. By six or seven, the obese child may already have more fat cells than a normal adult. In addition, each cell contains up to one and a half times as much fat as those of lean people.

Fat Cells: The Critical Periods

Dr. C. G. D. Brook of the University of London's Institute of Child Health reported in a medical journal in 1972 that the *most* sensitive period for the accumulation of irrevocable fat cells is between thirty weeks gestation (seven and a half months along in pregnancy) to one year. This means that some babies may be born with more than the normal number of fat cells, perhaps because of the makeup of their genes, *but more likely because in utero they were overfed.* In other words, they were born of fat mothers who overate, especially during pregnancy, and so bore babies who were fat at birth.

If a baby continues to be fat until a year of age, Brook feels, half the child's battle against overweight may already be lost.

According to Dr. Knittle, the critical periods in the development of fat cells, "with major consequences for one's adult weight," occur between birth and five years. He cites a previous study which "suggested two peaks for the onset of juvenile obesity, one between birth and four years and another at seven to eleven years."

The thin child has little change in her fat-cell count between the ages of two and ten, with most of her increase occurring before two, between nine and twelve, and again during the adolescent growth spurt. The cell development ends at about sixteen.

The fat child, on the other hand, continues to manufacture more and more cells throughout her entire childhood and at a much faster rate, thereby reaching adulthood with three or four times the normal number.

Important for parents to know is that the fat baby and child with excessive fat cells will never shed them, but will carry them around the rest of her life. Neither time nor diet will make them go away. They will shrink in size when their fat content is depleted, but they will always be there, ready to expand again. "It's as if the fat cells were sending out a signal to the brain saying 'Fill me up,' " says Dr. Hirsch.

"Why Did They Do That to Me?"

I remember a seventeen-year-old patient who complained bitterly to me about her weight problem. She had just read an article about fat cells in a magazine and said, "It's too late for me to do anything about my weight. It's hopeless. I've always been fat and so I have too many fat cells and I'll be fat till the day I die. Why did my parents do such a terrible thing to me?"

I explained to her that only in the last few years have we begun to understand the origins of fat. Her parents overfed her with the best of intentions. She was quite correct in assuming she had a superabundance of fat cells. However, I explained, these cells could be made smaller and lighter—and so she would be thinner—with proper diet and adequate exercise. True, it would take more effort for her and she'd have to be extra careful, but she could do it if she wanted to.

Happily, she took my advice and has managed, with effort, to slim down to a manageable weight.

The reason for the tendency of fat to cling to people with excess numbers of fat cells is still undiscovered, according to Dr. Knittle: "We know it is true, but we don't yet know why," he says.

Perhaps the explanation is the extreme efficiency with which the body with a high number of fat cells metabolizes food. Or perhaps the increased number of fat cells is related to increased appetite, somehow pushing up the "appestat" (which I'll discuss in more detail later).

It may work in this manner: Each adipose cell needs a certain level of fat content; it is "hungry" for it. Therefore, an individual with a tremendous number of these cells would tend to accumulate more total fat than normal.

This is probably why a person who has been far overweight as a child and has overproduced fat cells finds it extremely difficult to tolerate any sort of crash diet. On the other hand, the person who has only become fat as an adult, and so does not have a superabundance of these cells, can take a stringent diet more easily and more effectively.

However the fat cells work, the fact of the matter is that people with a larger than normal number of them have a more difficult time losing weight and keeping it off than other people because they can do it only by shrinking the cells which won't go away once they're there. The truth is that even when a fat person, child or adult, loses weight, she will always find it easier than others to regain the lost pounds.

Clearly then, if you don't want your child to grow up fat, her number of fat cells must remain normal. This can be accomplished only by keeping her thin right from the start.

If she already has developed too many cells, they can be kept from further increase if you don't *continue* to overfeed her.

I'll go on, in the next chapter, to discuss the third major cause of overweight in children, which is poor eating habits.

4

Ways Your Child Shouldn't Eat

The third major factor leading to overweight, after genes
and fat cells, is eating habits, which are established in the
very first year or two of a child's life. Once they're firmly
set, it's not easy to change them, as I explain to the parents
of all my newborns on their first visit to my office. When I
see parents who have already allowed their children to start
off down the path to fat, I urge them to make their stand
now before there's no turning back.

Far too many of our children grow up never having
learned how to eat properly. Overstuffed from the moment
they are born, they not only get fat but are often poorly
nourished despite the large amounts they consume. By the
time they are five or six, they have lost most of their
opportunity to grow up to be thin adults—unless a great
effort is made to change their course.

Too Much Food

One of my patients is Maria, a little girl of five who,
unfortunately, is not merely plump. At 102 pounds, she is
definitely obese. Her mother, who seems very concerned

about her weight, has discussed the problem with me many times, but my prognosis is that the child will always be fat. Why? Because the main preoccupation of the child's household is food. The chief form of entertainment is eating. Her mother, who is a marvelous cook and fat herself, is unable to cut down on her banquet-sized meals, to stop making rich desserts, or to resist filling her larder with fattening snacks. While one child in the family eats very little despite the environment, everyone else is far over-weight.

"It's heredity," says her mother. "Our family's always been overweight."

Perhaps the family has a genetic tendency toward fat, and probably everyone in it has many more than the average number of fat cells, but that little girl needn't be fat. Even with her background, which makes the job harder, she could grow up thin. But she has learned, and is constantly encouraged, to eat too much. And the prospects of a change now, I think, are minimal.

The Wrong Kinds of Food

Added to the modern habit of eating far too much for our energy needs is the growing emphasis in our culture on the *wrong* foods. Jamie is another child I know, a boy of nine who is not only fat but eats more "junk food" in a week than I eat in a year. "A poor eater" as an infant, according to his parents, Jamie was stuffed with too much milk from the start, fed solid foods long before they were necessary, bribed to eat every bite on his plate with the promise of candy and cookies.

Today he continues to eat poorly at meals and survives mainly on the high-calorie, non-nutritious foods his mother stocks in for him.

"What am I going to do?" she has complained to me. "That's all he really likes."

This mother's shortsightedness is aided and abetted by the advertising industry whose commercials during children's television programs continue to promote junk foods despite recent pressure from nutritionists to desist. One researcher, Joan Gussow, a nutrition instructor at Columbia University, monitored twenty-nine hours of network children's programs for a week, found that 82 percent of the commercials featured "anti-nutrition" foods. I, too, have watched hours of children's programs and I have never seen a commercial for string beans or apples, though a discouraging number for sugar-coated cereals and candy that won't melt in your hand.

The child who consumes an inordinate amount of "empty calories" may have her feelings of hunger satisfied, but she'll use them to replace the nutritious food she should be eating—and she'll probably get fat. But even if she doesn't, she will not be getting a good diet with enough of the necessary nutrients for growth and health.

Where Have All the Mealtimes Gone?

Because we all lead such complicated, busy lives today, it is becoming more and more difficult for families to eat meals together. Most of us, our children too, are on our own for breakfast. Lunches are grabbed at school or at work, often skipped altogether, or replaced by a series of snacks.

Dinners *may* be eaten together at the same time in the same place, but even these evening meals are becoming rare events in many households. And often they consist of prepared convenience foods whose nutritional value is doubtful.

In between these three so-called mealtimes, when the

nutrition taken in may be far below the proper standards because Mother—who used to plan all the food—is often no longer in control of what's being eaten, there is snacking. A lot of small nibbling, a little now, a little then, but rarely adding up to a worthwhile diet.

Are children learning good eating habits this way? Hardly.

Modifying Our Behavior

One of the most successful, currently popular methods of helping fat adults lose weight is called behavior modification. This method emphasizes the necessity of changing eating habits. For example, overweight people are helped to slow down their meals (studies have found that fat people eat inordinately fast and end up unsatisfied), to eat every bite sitting down in the same place (more calories are consumed if a person eats anywhere she happens to be, especially in front of the TV set); to take small portions on a small plate (less is eaten, it has been demonstrated, if one is faced with less visible food).

What parents can learn from this form of therapy is to avoid the necessity of it for our children. If we modify their behavior, teaching them the correct way to eat right from the beginning, they'll never get fat and they'll never need to retrain their eating habits.

Jimmy, the Bottomless Pit

Every day I hear from at least one mother that her child was born with a tremendous appetite and that's the reason she is overweight. Is appetite the same as hunger? When your baby cries, does it mean she wants to eat? How do you know when she's had enough? Why is one child's appetite so much larger than another's?

It's always been assumed that appetite is part of a person's inherent characteristics. Some babies, right from birth, do seem to be more voracious than others and, according to their mothers, are "always hungry." A mother just last week assured me that little Jimmy, aged four months and gaining too rapidly, was a bottomless pit, crying constantly and unremittingly for his bottle. "What can I do?" she asked. "I can't let him starve. He wants it."

Mrs. G., another mother, came to my office recently to complain once more that Debby, now twelve, had the appetite of a truck driver and promptly ate every cookie in the package as soon as her mother brought it home from the market. "I buy a chocolate layer cake or a blueberry pie for dessert, and Debby eats the entire thing if I don't watch out," she said. "She was always like that."

Needless to say, Debby is fat.

Appetite vs. Hunger

"Appetite" is one's desire for and anticipation of food, and it is not the same as "hunger." Hunger is the physical need to eat, signaled by contractions of the stomach and the lowering of blood sugar levels. Though there have not, so far as I know, been any tests on appetite vs. hunger made on children, there have been a number involving adults. All of these show that fat people's appetites are not closely related to their real hunger, that they eat for other reasons.

One project conducted by Dr. Stanley Schacter, professor of psychology at Columbia University, studied the cues for eating. A group of subjects, half of them fat and half of them thin, were asked to arrive at the laboratory at lunchtime without having first eaten lunch. Informed that the purpose of the test was to judge the flavor of various kinds of crackers (though the real intent was to measure appetites), half of the group (mixed fat and thin) were given sandwiches to eat. The other half was given nothing. Then they were all provided with the crackers and told to eat as many as they wished.

The results were that the thin subjects ate more crackers when they were hungry, while the fat subjects ate just as many whether they were actually hungry or not.

Another of Schacter's research projects was related to time. Separated into two groups and seated in rooms with wall clocks just before dinnertime, fat and thin students were told the experiment would measure physiological responses. Though fifty minutes, the same amount of time, elapsed for both groups during the experiment, the clock in one room was set to run fifteen minutes slow and the clock in the other room was set to run thirty minutes fast. Thus, the first group thought only a little time had passed, while the other believed much more time had gone by.

At the end, each group was casually offered crackers while they completed some meaningless written forms. The obese subjects ate more when they thought it was about dinnertime than when they thought it was not yet time to be hungry—the opposite of the thin subjects. In other words, the fat people ate because they thought it was time to eat, not because they were hungry.

Dr. Henry A. Jordan, assistant professor of psychiatry at the University of Pennsylvania School of Medicine, and his colleagues recently conducted an experiment in the university cafeteria. Unknown to the subjects, the researchers watched fat people as they chose their lunches, and discovered that they picked rich, high-calorie desserts when these desserts were temptingly placed at the front of the shelves.

Conversely, they tended to choose low-calorie desserts

much more often when the shelves were rearranged so that the rich desserts were moved to the back where they were not so visible or available.

Another study showed fat people eating more when they felt fear, rather than less as a thin person does, while other research has related appetite to the sight of food, the taste, the smell, and so forth. All studies demonstrated that fat people respond inappropriately to food, that their appetites do not relate to real physiological hunger. They require signals from the outside to know when to eat and how much.

Their "appestats," the internal control mechanisms which tell us when to eat and when to stop in order to take in the right amount of food to keep our bodies going, were not working properly.

Are Some Babies Hungrier?

It's been theorized that some babies are born with appestat mechanisms that are set higher than others, giving them bigger appetites, and that the number of fat cells a child possesses affects his appetite, pushing the appestat higher as they multiply. For these reasons, some children would naturally want more food than others.

My experience is that newborn babies' appetites don't actually vary as much as their mothers think. I think different mothers react differently to signals from their babies. Some think that every time their babies fret or cry they're hungry. So they feed them and feed them and feed them. The babies are trained to overeat and they also learn that food is the answer to any stress or discomfort.

Some mothers think their babies can't be healthy if they aren't fat, so they stuff them with as much food as they will accept. Other mothers don't want to take the time to find out what really is bothering their fretting infants, or to cuddle or play at an inconvenient time, so they feed them to keep them quiet. And some feel that as long as the babies will accept food they must need and want it.

How Much Is Enough?

Mothers always ask how they are to know when their babies have eaten enough. My answer is that the only real way to know whether they're getting enough—or too much—is by the rate of their weight gain. A baby needs as much food as will allow her to grow at a normal rate.

The same is true of an older child, including the adolescent. A child who is gaining too rapidly is obviously eating too much for the amount of energy she uses.

Knowing when enough is enough, when to stop eating, as well as what to eat, is something that's learned by a child very early in life. She is taught how to eat by the person who feeds her and by the environment she grows in. She learns by example.

However it is developed and nurtured, an appetite unrelated to true hunger is usually a lifetime possession. Much better to help your child develop a normal healthy appetite in the first place.

The last major factor leading to obesity is the sedentary life our affluent, mechanized society has created. Few of us do enough exercise and so we do not burn up enough calories. This subject will be discussed in the next chapter.

I think it's clear that there are a number of causes of perennial overweight and that these are interconnected and overlap. We can't do a thing about the genetic component, but we surely can handle the rest.

5

Exercise Does *Help*

"But, Doctor," fifteen-year-old Liz said to me when I urged her to get some exercise every day, "I heard you've got to walk thirteen hours just to lose one pound. I'd rather go on a diet. Besides, exercise makes me hungry."

Liz, who was about twenty pounds too heavy and very unhappy about it, was discussing her weight problem with me. I agreed that it certainly was ridiculous to expect anyone to walk thirteen hours at a stretch. Or to ride a bike for seven and a half hours, or swim steadily for five.

"But," I explained, "you don't have to get your exercise all at once. If you ride your bike for *half an hour* every evening after dinner, in two weeks you'll have done your seven hours. In a year that takes care of twenty-six pounds of fat. If you walk at a fast clip for a half an hour a day, you'll lose a pound in less than three weeks, or seventeen pounds in a year. Swimming, if you really swim and don't just float around, will do it in only ten days.

"Exercise," I told her, "is the only way you can burn up the calories you eat. Sure, you can lose weight if you go on a very strict diet, but you and I both know all about the diets you've tried already. You could do it by exercise alone, too, but it's much simpler and quicker to cut down on your food

37

a little and increase your exercise a little at the same time.

"Not only that," I added, "but exercise will tone your body up, your muscles will be firmer, you'll lose a lot of flab, and you'll look and feel a lot better."

Liz, who was determined to fit into her swimsuit by summer, managed to shed fifteen pounds with the help of exercise by the time I saw her again, five months later.

Fat People Exercise Less

Almost everyone thinks, as Liz did, that exercise is too tough and a waste of time, and that overeating is the only reason people get fat. Food *does* put on the pounds, but only if the calories taken in are not expended in activity. There must be a balance of calorie intake and energy output to keep weight stable. If your child eats more food than he requires to keep his body going, he will gain. If he eats less, he will lose.

Jean Mayer has flatly stated that "probably no single factor is more frequently responsible for the development of obesity . . . than lack of physical exercise. . . . Repeated studies have shown that the great majority of obese adolescents eat less than the average non-obese adolescents of the same sex. The inactivity . . . easily accounts for the calories which permit excessive fat deposition."

He and his colleagues at Harvard found in a study made of a group of overweight girls that on the average they ate *less* than a thin control group, but spent only a *third* as much time in physical activity. In another project, movies were taken of fat and thin girls swimming and playing tennis. They revealed that the fat girls tended to plant themselves in one spot on the court, taking a swing at the ball if it happened to come near them, and spent most of their time in the pool floating around, taking a stroke now and then.

Despite that, they honestly thought they were exercising.

A well-known experiment a few years back measured the number of steps taken by two groups of housewives, one fat and one thin, as they went about their normal household activities. Pedometers attached to their legs revealed that the lean housewives walked twice as far as the fat ones though attending to the very same things.

Dr. Hilda Bruch of Baylor College of Medicine in Texas, who has also extensively studied overweight children, noted that out of 160 obese youngsters studied, 76 percent of the boys and 88 percent of the girls were almost totally inactive. Adds Dr. Ruth L. Huenemann of the University of California School of Public Health, "The problem . . . is not eating too much. Rather it is eating too much for the energy expended. The generally low level of physical activity that appears to be characteristic of American youth and the consequent low caloric need make increased activity an essential part of the regimens for obesity prevention and control."

Farmers have always taken advantage of the fact that inactivity results in fat. Penning their animals to fatten them up for market, they know that the restricted beasts will continue to eat just as much as they did before and therefore gain weight.

And all of us have always known that it's easier to gain weight in the winter, when we get less exercise than we do in the warmer weather.

The "Sluggish Metabolism" Myth

A certain amount of energy is consumed by the body merely by being alive—the beating of the heart, breathing, digestion, maintaining body temperature, and other functions. This phenomenon is called basal energy, or basal metabolism, and *it varies little* from person to person, fat or thin—no matter what you've heard! The so-called "sluggish metabolism" or "sluggish thyroid," blamed by so many overweight people for their extra pounds, is very rare.

It is not true that thin people at rest burn up calories faster than fat people (with a very few exceptions); what *is* true, however, is that thin people move *more* and move *faster,* thereby increasing their caloric expenditure.

There *is* one hormone that is affected by being overweight and this adds to the difficulties of a person who becomes fat. Overeating stimulates the production of insulin from the pancreas and this insulin acts as a storage hormone. It helps to store fat in the cells and contributes to maintaining it there. With a high level of circulating insulin which fights to keep the fat in the cells, overweight people find it hard to lose pounds. There is, however, a bright side to this picture—this overproduction of insulin in the obese person is completely reversible. Once weight is brought down to normal, the insulin level also returns to normal.

It has clearly been shown that exercise effectively lowers the elevated level of insulin. Therefore, it is doubly important for the overweight individual to exercise, to use up calories and to lower his insulin level.

Another small amount of energy is used in the utilization of food by the body.

The energy expended in physical activity, the movement of the muscles, is the most important for our purposes because it's the kind we can do something about. And the amount of energy expended makes an enormous difference in determining whether we are fat or thin. The range of daily caloric output varies in different people by the thousands of calories. In adolescent boys, for example, it can go from 2,800 calories for the extremely inactive youngster to more than 6,000 for the athlete, according to Dr. Mayer. Studies by Mayer have clearly shown that people engaged in heavy labor burn up tremendous numbers of calories while sedentary workers use up comparatively few.

In this affluent, increasingly urbanized and mechanized society, we are all sitting around more and moving less. In fact, the National Adult Physical Fitness Survey reported that 45 percent of Americans engage in no physical activity for exercise at all. With a high priority on saving steps and effort, few of us walk when we can ride, climb stairs when we can take the elevator, wash dishes or mow the lawn when we've got machines to do it for us. While our ancestors spent most of their day at physical labor, most of us today get exercise only when we make a special point of it.

Inactive people, children too, need less food than active people do. Because as a nation the amount of exercise we get has decreased so steadily in recent years, the Food and Nutrition Board of the National Research Council has accordingly steadily reduced its recommended daily allowance of calories with each succeeding revision.

Help for Tired Mothers

The problem of inactivity vs. weight gain begins early in life. In our society, from the time babies are born they are protected from exertion, pushed around in strollers, confined in playpens, driven around in cars. With overcrowding and growing street traffic, less open space, and fewer play areas, mothers make appointments for their children to "play" with each other. That, I've found, usually means sitting in front of the television set munching pretzels. Preschool children, according to a recent survey, watch TV an average of five hours a day, a five-hour slot during which they might otherwise have been running around. How often I've heard mothers of preschool children say, "Thank God for TV. It's the only time he's quiet and I can get some work done."

Some children, of course, are naturally more active than others, and I've discovered few mothers who don't prefer a nice quiet baby who stays put and doesn't require a lot of attention. After all, he's less of a handful than the baby who's into everything and loves to take off on explorations. But while his adventurous brother is using up a lot of energy, and undoubtedly remaining nicely thin, the inactive baby will tend to get fat. If he gets fat at this early age, he may well be fat the rest of his life, not only because he will develop a superabundance of fat cells, but also because he will become set in his inactive ways.

Even small babies need a chance to exercise; they love to be tossed about, have their legs moved, to be stood up on their feet, walked and bounced. They're not as fragile as most people think and they won't break, assuming, of course, they're handled gently. Nor will they turn out bowlegged. If the baby is happy being exercised, the activity can't harm him (despite what Grandma may say).

Let Your Baby Move Around

As they grow and develop, babies should always be encouraged to creep and crawl, be given a chance to climb and pull themselves up freely, and not be confined in little seats and carriages more than necessary. This will develop their coordination, improve muscle tone and skills as well as help them to efficiently utilize the food they eat.

I try at every opportunity to influence the mothers of my small patients to let their toddlers get around under their own steam. Walking is great exercise and doesn't require a bit of equipment. I urge them: Take your little ones places where they can run and climb. Use the stroller only when you must and leave the car behind when you can. Walking, I tell them, is good for *you* too.

With appropriate safety precautions, of course, let young children ride their bikes, play ball, roller skate, climb trees or jungle gyms, or just plain run around. Once they start school, they can walk to school under most circumstances and back home again as well. Many mothers seem to think that a bus or the car is a necessity if school is more than a few blocks away. Nonsense. Children are quite capable of making it almost anywhere.

"Gerald Gets So Tired."

Seven-year-old Gerald's mother arrived at my office late for an appointment and most apologetic. There had been a big mixup with the car pool and she'd had to pick up her younger child unexpectedly.

"That's too bad," I said. "How far is it to school from your house?"

"Nine blocks," she said.

"From now on," I suggested gently, "why don't you let Gerald walk back and forth to school? From what you've told me, he's not much of an athlete, and we both know he's overweight. He needs the exercise."

"But he's so young," she protested. "And he gets so tired."

"He's old enough to walk nine blocks," I said. "And there's no reason for him to get tired—he's perfectly healthy. Once he gets used to it, he'll be just fine. You'll see." She later reported that my forecast had proved entirely accurate.

Many youngsters who get enough exercise in their preschool years turn sedentary, and overweight, once they start school and spend a good part of their day sitting down.

Add to that the fact that physical-education programs in the schools are often woefully inadequate and you may have to take the exercise problems into your own parental hands.

Exercise for Health

Exercise habits, like eating habits, are hard to change. A child who doesn't move much will undoubtedly turn into an adolescent and adult who won't move much either. At that point, his immobility will cause additional problems besides fat.

"Exercise isn't just to keep the weight down," says noted specialist Dr. Denton Cooley of the Texas Heart Institute. "It keeps all the muscles including the heart muscle in tone and this is a very important safeguard. By exercising, we develop collateral coronary circulation." This collateral circulation is very important in protecting against heart attacks.

There is another value to exercise. It has been shown to lower blood cholesterol levels and this is always a good idea as elevated cholesterol is associated with elevated blood pressure and incidence of heart attacks. This probably explains why members of the Masai tribe of Africa, though they eat a diet very high in fats, have neither elevated cholesterol levels nor many heart attacks—they walk an average of twenty-six miles a day.

Once a child has become heavy, moving around becomes harder for him to manage and he becomes even less interested in exercise, more self-conscious about looking clumsy and uncoordinated and unattractive. The problem thus becomes a vicious circle.

Because it's not a simple matter to change patterns that have been firmly established since childhood, it's much better to establish them the right way in the first place.

How to Get Jimmy Going

Parents often say to me, "I know exercise is important, but what can I do? Jimmy isn't interested in sports."

I tell them they themselves have got to get involved. Subtly. Orders to go out and run around the block or ride a bike three miles to the swimming pool won't work. But gentle encouragement, and their own participation, may. Here's what I recommend.

• Nothing works better in interesting a youngster in an activity than a family outing. If you've made exercise a family affair right from the beginning, all of you going off on bike rides, ice skating, skiing, bowling, hiking, swimming, whatever, as a group, you wouldn't be reading this now. But if you haven't and you're searching for ways to get *your* Jimmy going, start now, before his desire to sit down becomes irrevocably stronger than his desire to run.

• Encourage your child to become proficient at a sport because, once he does, he'll have a lot more fun doing it. If necessary, arrange for lessons. Most children, for example, enjoy swimming. Let yours develop some expertise by taking lessons at the local pool.

• Buy necessary equipment if you can. A bike, a basketball, roller skates, a hockey stick, a football helmet, a tennis racquet. A moderate investment of this sort will pay off many times over.

• Though most children need do no back-breaking work as they did in former days, they certainly can do chores around the house, run errands, do their own traveling. Making beds and sweeping the floor, washing windows, going to the store, mowing the lawn, and raking leaves all use up calories. While I don't suggest you work your child mercilessly, both the responsibility and the exercise will be good for him.

• Get together with other parents and investigate the physical-education program at your school. If it seems to be inadequate, doesn't provide active participation for *every* child *every* day, protest. Try to organize recreation programs that include sports.

• Push *carryover* sports, sports that can be continued all of your child's life. While football, hockey, basketball are all fine exercise, it's not easy to organize a team when you're forty years old. And, from a practical point of view, even the kids don't find it possible to get up a football team every afternoon. Sports that don't require great numbers of people, or even *anyone* else, are the ones that last, like biking, swimming, Ping-Pong, tumbling, tennis. I took up tennis when I was ten and I have played at least twice a week ever since. Not only has tennis kept my weight down, but it has been a source of a great deal of fun and pleasure. I hope I can continue to play forever.

• Activity that's fun, like games, is more likely to have long-lasting interest for your child than toe-touching or sit-up exercises. Exercises are great, and a half hour a day can work wonders, but if you've known a child of any age who's kept at them longer than a few days or a week, I would be amazed. The many overweight adolescents I see invariably tell me they're going to embark on an exercise program of this kind and I encourage them to do so, but I can think of only a couple who've kept at it long enough for real results. It becomes a bore and so hardly ever works out.

Too Embarrassed to Exercise

On the other hand, *very* fat children often are too embarrassed to be seen in a swimsuit or pedaling a bike in front of the neighbors. Perhaps youngsters will exercise at home if you can all do it together. Or perhaps the investment in a Ping-Pong table or a stationary bicycle will get them started.

Soon after I started my practice, I spent a couple of summers as the doctor in a summer camp. I vividly remember an overweight eleven-year-old boy who made constant trips to the infirmary complaining of earaches and asking to be excused from swimming.

It didn't take long for me to realize that there was nothing wrong with his ears, but that he was terribly embarrassed about the way he looked in swimming trunks. I couldn't excuse him from water activity all summer long, so I did the next best thing I could think of. I told him to wear a T-shirt along with his swimsuit (and checked with the counselor so there would be no remarks about it), to jump right in the lake as soon as he was allowed, and never to stop moving, swimming as vigorously as he could every single second he was in the water. I promised him he'd end up a lot thinner by the time he went home.

And I was right. He was noticeably thinner and a lot happier.

Sometimes the unexpected works. I discussed an exercise program with a family that included a grossly overweight twelve-year-old boy. No matter what his parents did to interest him in exercise, no luck. They bought him weight-lifting equipment, a basketball, took him to the pool every Saturday. His lethargy was so ingrained by the time his parents became concerned that the situation looked hopeless.

But a few months later, the boy appeared in my office eight pounds lighter. I was amazed. I asked him what had happened. He couldn't think of anything that had changed; he was eating the same foods and he still couldn't care less about sports.

Just as he was leaving, he said, "By the way, Dr. Eden, I've got a new dog." It turned out he not only had a new dog but he had a *big* new dog that needed lots of running. It was his job to walk the dog and he was doing it, three times a day.

If you can get your child to start exercising, you'll soon see results too. A little at a time, maybe a half hour a day more than before, is all you need expect because, as I told Liz, it all adds up.

Fat Will *Disappear with Exercise*

The myth that you can't lose weight by exercising is one myth that's got to go because exercise does burn off surplus calories. What's more, it burns them off faster for a fat person than a lean one—he'll use more energy per minute doing the very same thing.

To show you what's possible, here are the caloric values per hour of some common activities and the *weekly* results of one hour per day of the exercise:

CALORIC VALUES OF COMMON ACTIVITIES

	Per Hour	Weight Loss Per Week (Approx.)
Walking slowly	170	$\frac{1}{3}$ pound
Walking rapidly	350	$\frac{3}{4}$ pound
Jogging	450	1 pound
Running	900	$1\frac{3}{4}$ pounds
Swimming	685	$1\frac{1}{2}$ pounds
Roller skating	650	$1\frac{1}{3}$ pounds
Biking	500	1 pound
Skiing	650	$1\frac{1}{3}$ pounds
Tennis	500	1 pound

In order for a person to use up 500 calories' worth of fat a day, or a pound a week (3,500 calories), which is usually the most a child should lose if his growth isn't to be adversely threatened, he could eat exactly the same as he does now but add an hour a day of bike riding or forty minutes of active swimming.

A bonus: there's evidence that because metabolism is revved up by the exercise, it continues to work more efficiently even after the activity has ceased, burning up even more calories than the hourly table would indicate.

But better, for most children, than trying to keep up a strenuous daily exercise pattern to which they are utterly unaccustomed is to combine a *slight* increase in exercise with a *slight* decrease in food. This produces the maximum results in the shortest time. For example, if Liz ate 250 calories less food a day (the equivalent of two cans of soda or five chocolate-chip cookies) and also biked 250 calories' worth (a half hour or so), by the end of a week she'd have shed that same pound.

Most youngsters needn't change their ways even that much. Unless they are really obese, all they need to do is lower their caloric surplus a tiny amount so that they will not lose weight but also not gain, letting their height catch up with their weight. Perhaps only 100 calories' worth of diet cutback (one can of soda) and 100 calories' worth of exercise (fifteen minutes of bike riding) will do the job. This small adjustment in calories is easy to accomplish and easy to maintain and will work. This is the key to success. There is no hardship or deprivation for the child and it becomes a way of life.

I asked one of my patients, sixteen-year-old Susan, to switch from a coke with her lunch, if not to skimmed milk then to a diet soda, and to walk at a fast clip back and forth to school every day instead of getting a ride from a friend. It worked very nicely.

Not only is it less effort to tackle the problem with both diet and exercise, but research has shown that *98 percent of the weight lost by a combination of the two is likely to be fat tissue,* while only 75 percent of it is fat when only diet is changed.

And, according to a report by Drs. A. K. Dudleston and M. Bennion in the *Journal of the American Dietetic Association,* the combination of exercise and diet gets weight off about 10 percent more quickly than diet alone.

An Exploded Myth: "Exercise Makes You Hungry."

Another myth is the widely held belief that exercise makes you hungry. Contrary to what you may think, this is simply not so. In fact, the appetite may actually drop during the early stages of unaccustomed exercise. Exercising to the point of exhaustion—which I do not recommend—can turn off the appetite almost completely. And, says Dr. Jules Hirsch of Rockefeller University, exercise has a "euphoriant effect" that cuts down one's need to turn to food for emotional satisfaction.

That exercise is effective as a weight reducer was undeniably demonstrated by one of the Mayer group's experimental programs conducted in a large public school in Massachusetts. Several hundred obese children and adolescents were helped to lose weight—and keep it off—"essentially through stepped-up daily physical activity."

So, if you can interest your youngster, preferably from the beginning of his life but starting at whatever age, in using his muscles regularly, you'll be doing him a tremendous service. If he's thin, he'll stay that way. If he's overweight, physical activity *has* to help him become thin and healthy.

6

The Food Your Child Should Eat

My patient was twelve and without a doubt she was fat. I was discussing her weight with her and her mother and I asked them to keep a record for a week of the food the girl ate. The next week, when the mother brought the record to my office, we were both shocked when we went over it. Instead of a nutritious, well-balanced diet, Joann turned out to be consuming a tremendous number of calories with very little high-quality body-building food. In fact, I concluded, if this was what she ate normally, and it seemed to be, she was actually malnourished.

The Typical American Is Not Well Fed

I'm sure most parents assume, especially if their youngsters are overweight, that they're feeding their children well. But that is not necessarily true. The truth is that the typical American family today is not well fed.

While there is no shortage of good food in the United States, nor, for most of us, the money to buy it, our diet is growing steadily poorer, far too high in calories, most of them fats and carbohydrates, with a higher proportion of quick pre-prepared foods, a continual round of non-nutritious snacks, and fewer real honest-to-goodness meals.

According to Dr. Paul Fine, a psychologist who made a study of food habits for a group of large food manufacturers, three out of four families do not eat breakfast together, and many eat no breakfast at all. Lunches are usually eaten on the run and have no relationship to good nutrition, while dinner takes place "as seldom as three days a week or less" and may take only twenty minutes or so to eat.

What that means is that our children are often basically on their own when it comes to the food they eat, especially when they become teen-agers, and that the mother no longer has much control over their choices.

Snacking: A National Habit

Snacking, says Dr. Fine, is "the American pattern from early morning to bedtime." Instead of three square meals a day, "the American mainstream feeds on Oreos, peanut butter, Crisco, TV dinners, cake mix, macaroni and cheese, Pepsi and Coke, pizzas, Jell-O, hamburgers, Rice-a-Roni, Spaghetti-O's, pork and beans, Heinz catsup and instant coffee."

Even so-called meals are frequently really snacks. According to James L. Breeling of the American Medical Association's department of foods and nutrition, "The typical American mother today doesn't know what her family is eating . . . she just restocks supplies and fixes the meals that account for only one third to one half of her family's daily food intake.

"Of the food consumed at home," he says, "a significant percentage is of the snack and pre-prepared convenience variety. . . . Nutritionists and consumer advocates are concerned that pleasant but nutritionally inadequate foods will find too large a place in the American diet, in the guise of snack foods, fun foods, and foods inappropriately used by the consumer as meal replacements."

Said Helen D. Ullrich, editor of the *Journal of Nutrition Education*, at a recent hearing of the U.S. Senate Select Committee on Nutrition, "Obviously, the choices of food that people make are costing this country unnecessary dollars in medical bills, loss of time at work and leisure. . . . When you have 8,000 items to choose from in a supermarket, instinct will not guarantee a wise choice."

Because you would not be reading this book if you were not concerned with bringing up slim, healthy children, I would like to discuss with you the nutritional elements which must be present in their daily diets.

Understanding Good Nutrition

Nutrition is a subject which is only beginning to be understood by more than a few people, including physicians, so it is no wonder we have become a nation of poor eaters. When I went to medical school, we did not study nutrition except for the vitamin-deficiency diseases such as scurvy and rickets; only recently have some medical schools begun to include nutrition training in their programs, the number doubling, to 42 percent, between November 1973 and November 1974.

Granted, nutrition does not seem like a very thrilling subject—and I've found most mothers would rather not think about it too seriously—but it's important that you not shortchange your children. They can be overweight and still poorly nourished. In fact, overweight children are *more* likely to be undernourished than those of normal weight because they tend to be addicted to trash foods.

Babies and very small children are, in general, well fed

(though perhaps too much) by mothers (or mother substitutes) who follow doctors' orders carefully for the first year or two. But the trend toward easy meals begins early and escalates as the children reach school age, probably reaching its peak by the time they become adolescents.

It's Your Job to Choose the Food

While I certainly understand why many women no longer want to invest so much time and effort in cooking and serving, it's important to remember that growing children (and that includes teen-agers who are growing faster than they have at any time since they were two) require food that will make them healthy, sturdy adults who will live a normal life span. They are not very likely to choose the right food on their own—carrots never taste as good to untrained palates as chocolate-fudge cookies, and vending machines never sell grapefruit. Nor is good food advertised with as much fervor as sugar-coated, artificially colored cereal or marshmallow-filled cupcakes.

Today there are almost 10,000 different supermarket items, with about 60 percent of them processed or convenience foods. Because many prepared, processed, refined foods lose much of their nutrient content, and because it's practically impossible to tell what nourishment many convenience foods actually contain, I think there must be renewed reliance on the originals—*real* unadulterated fresh foods. Aside from the nutritional aspects, we know that fresh foods will not contain hidden calories, which will only make our children fat, or chemical additives, which may affect their eventual health.

Facts About Food

Let me begin with some simple facts I'm sure you know and remind you of the proper diet for children and adolescents (as well as adults).

• Food is the source of all our energy. We need it to live, to fuel the body's functions, and—as children—for growth.

• The three main elements in food are carbohydrates, fats and proteins, supplemented by vitamins, minerals and water (plus roughage which is necessary for proper digestion). A well-balanced diet contains adequate amounts of all of these.

• From the food a child eats, his body chooses what is needed for the function of certain organs or parts of the body, discarding or storing the excess. But it cannot manufacture or compensate for nutrients which are not supplied in sufficient amounts, and so a wide variety of foods is necessary to provide everything a growing body requires.

• Vitamin supplements are useful, and essential when insufficient amounts of certain foods are eaten, but they cannot be used as replacements for food. There are over fifty nutritional factors our bodies need and they are best supplied by food.

• If your child is brought up eating nutritious well-balanced meals, having learned good eating habits from the beginning, it is doubtful he will ever get fat.

• Eating healthily is a learned skill. It does not come naturally. Parents must teach their children what to eat, making good eating habits so ingrained that they will continue for the rest of their lives.

• Almost all foods provide energy which is measured in "calories." The most calories are found in foods that are rich in fats or carbohydrates (sugars and starches).

• When a diet furnishes more calories than the body needs, the excess supply is stored in the body as fat. When it furnishes fewer calories than the body uses, the body uses the stored supply for energy resulting in weight loss.

What Is a Well-Balanced Diet?

Every child, if he's to have a healthy diet, should eat minimum daily amounts of food from what nutritionists call the four basic food groups:

1. Meat Group: This includes meat, poultry and fish; with alternates of eggs, dry beans, lentils and peas; soybeans, nuts, peanut butter, etc. It provides protein, iron and the B vitamins.
Servings: Two or more a day (two to three ounces per serving, not counting bones) of lean meat, poultry or fish. Or a per-serving equivalent of two eggs, one cup of dry beans, peas or lentils or soybeans, four tablespoons peanut butter.

2. Vegetable-Fruit Group: All vegetables and fruits. This provides vitamins, in particular Vitamins A and C, and natural sugars and starches.
Servings: Four or more daily, which should include at least one serving of a Vitamin C source (citrus, cantaloupe, strawberries, broccoli, Brussels sprouts, green pepper etc.). And one serving at least every other day of a Vitamin A source (dark green and deep yellow vegetables, cantaloupe, apricots, sweet potatoes, etc.). One serving: $\frac{1}{2}$ cup of fruit or vegetable.

3. Milk Group: Milk (whole, skim, evaporated, dry, buttermilk), cheese and milk products. Nutritive elements include protein, calcium and phosphorus, riboflavin (Vitamin B-2), Vitamin A and, if fortified, Vitamin D.

Servings: Children under 9: two to three 8-ounce cups.
            Children 9 to 12: three
            Teen-agers: four
Part of the milk may be replaced by cheese, ice cream, yogurt.

4. Bread-Cereal Group: All breads and cereals that are whole grain, enriched or restored. Also pasta, rice, grits, cornmeal, etc. These give your child protein, carbohydrates, iron and several vitamins.

Servings: Four or more servings.

One serving: one slice of bread, one ounce ready-to-eat cereal, $\frac{1}{2}$ to $\frac{3}{4}$ cup cooked cereal, cornmeal, pasta, rice, grits.

Along with these basic groups, you will undoubtedly serve your children other foods such as sugars, flours, oils and fats which are energy sources and flavor enhancers.

What These Foods Do

Briefly, here are the chief values to your child of the nutritive elements in these foods.

• Protein: Needed for growth and repair of body tissues, helps production of antibodies that fight off infection, production of enzymes and hormones.

• Fats: These provide a concentrated source of energy and add flavor to foods, carry Vitamins A, D, E and K along with essential fatty acids, protect vital organs by cushioning them.

• Carbohydrates: These starches and sugars found in grains, fruits, vegetables, table sugar, etc., are our major source of energy.

• Water: Necessary for all the processes of digestion and an essential part of all tissues. Also supplies minerals.

• Minerals and iron: For strong bones and teeth,

healthy circulatory, muscular and nervous systems, blood hemoglobin, etc.

• Vitamin A: Important in eye function, helps keep the skin and mucous membranes healthy and resistant to infection.

• B Vitamins: These release food energy, are important to the health of the digestive system, nervous system, skin, blood hemoglobin.

• Vitamin C: Necessary for healthy collagen, which is the cementing material holding body cells together; for healing; healthy blood vessels, etc.

• Vitamin D: Important for strong bones and teeth, as well as growth, for without it the body cannot absorb calcium and phosphorus. It also is supplied by sunshine on bare skin.

• Vitamin E: Its exact role is not fully understood, though it is known to be essential in maintaining body tissues.

• Vitamin K: Essential for the manufacture of a substance that helps the blood to clot.

• Roughage: Not a nutrient, but important for healthy teeth and gums, efficient digestion. Found in fruits, vegetables and grains. Note: Three British physicians have recently reported that many diseases of Western civilization, such as appendicitis, cancer of the colon, and diverticulitis, have appeared only in the last century. They believe this is because of "the removal of indigestible fiber from the carbohydrate foods that constitute the major part of our diet." The doctors recommend we eat more unprocessed carbohydrates, especially whole-grain foods.

What We Actually Eat

In 1972, the last year for which we have U.S. Department of Agriculture figures, the average American ate nearly three-quarters of a ton of food. But over 30 percent of the total calories we took in were snack foods, many of them completely non-nutritious.

To illustrate my point, here are the approximate caloric values of some popular snacks.

Orange soda (8 ounces) 126
Chocolate popsicle......................... 106
Candy-coated chocolate candies (1) ounce) 130
Potato chips (1 ounce) 158
Peanut brittle (1 ounce) 125
Coconut cookies (5) 390
Pecan brownies (2 ounces) 224
Chocolate chip cookies (5) 250
Ring Ding (2½ ounces) 366
Fried apple pie (4 ounces) 363
Frosted cereal flakes (1 cup) 143
Fruit drink (8 ounces) 110

See page 209 for the caloric values of more snack foods.
Healthy low-calorie snacks include:

1 large carrot............................. 20
2 8-inch stalks celery 10
½ cantaloupe.............................. 50
½ banana................................. 40
1 medium apple........................... 70
½ cup tomato juice 20
1 cup skimmed milk 90
1 cup popcorn 40
1 slice whole-wheat bread.................. 55
1 cup puffed wheat 55

• In averaging the American diet as a whole, each of us takes in 3,200 calories a day, which means that many of us are eating more than that, while about 2,400 calories should be plenty for almost anyone not doing hard labor.

• The typical American eats more than 100 pounds of

refined sugar a year, with teen-agers averaging much more. Most of this comes from manufactured foods with almost a quarter of that in beverages. Carbohydrates, which include both sugars and starches, provide 40 to 50 percent of the average diet.

• It's been estimated that in 1972 each of us ate five pounds of chemicals (3,000 varieties) added to food to preserve it, flavor it, or color it.

• Forty to 50 percent of our average diet consists of fat, most of it animal fat. We should aim for 35 percent or less.

• Our pattern of eating, with its high sugar, starch, fat (mainly saturated) content will in the long run cause gradually accumulating and irreparably damaging changes in the body.

• Almost all infants (97 percent) are fed solid foods before the age of two months. Twenty percent get them by the age of one week. This is *much* too early. Three months is the minimum age for starting solids.

A Few Recommendations

• No food should be cut *out* of a normal diet, though some should be cut *down*. In my "non-diet," for example, I do not recommend that a child eat no sugar. Sugar is needed for quick energy. But I think that our children consume far too much of it, which is why fatproofing the house is so essential. Clear the house of the foods that contribute high numbers of calories but little or no nutrition. That includes many packaged breakfast cereals, which, according to a petition sponsored by a group of consumer groups including the American Public Health Association, may well contain 40 to 50 percent sugar.

• I am not recommending cutting out starches because

they, too, provide energy and nutrition, and are not necessarily fattening. A medium-size potato without butter or gravy, for example, contains no more calories than an ounce of good steak or a large orange and it provides iron and vitamins. Grains of all kinds, which go into bread and pasta, rice, and corn, make up one of the basic necessary foods. I do recommend cutting down on starches if an inordinate amount is eaten.

• Many parents feel that the more protein their children eat, the better. Not true, because most of our protein has a high fat content and only a certain amount of protein can be utilized by the body. Children should get *enough* protein (12 to 15 percent of the daily caloric intake) but not too much.

• The foods American children tend to shun are fruits and vegetables, and these are what they must learn to eat if they're to be healthy as well as thin. I recommend raw fruit as much as possible—or cooked without excess sugar. And vegetables eaten raw or quickly cooked in a little water.

• Because many processed, refined foods have vitamins "restored" to them, many people assume they are just as healthy as natural foods. However, some elements cannot be restored and in the processing needed roughage is often lost. The restoration process is also expensive, and that cost is passed on to *you*.

Easy on the Salt

A few words about salt must be said here. Salt is a flavor enhancer which should be used in moderation only, because it may contribute to the development of high blood pressure and kidney disease. Though you may not be concerned now about the possible eventuality of your child developing these problems, I think you should be.

A person's desire for salt is usually developed when he is very young and stays with him forever, with the average American consuming five to twenty times the estimated daily requirement. My own love of salt goes back to when I was a child and my mother bribed me to eat my oatmeal by promising me delicious salty foods like pickles and olives if I finished it. My mother tells me she always loved salt and assumed I would too. Today I'd rather sprinkle salt on my hot cereal than sugar, and I have an almost irresistible desire to sprinkle salt on everything I eat.

The mother who sprinkles salt on baby food because she thinks it helps the taste, or because she likes a lot of salt herself, is doing the baby a disservice. The salt used in normal cooking is plenty, though very bland food that contains no perceptible salt to begin with, like eggs, can receive a light-handed sprinkle.

Many prepared baby foods are, I think, unnecessarily overseasoned and you'd do better, if you have the time and the inclination, to make your own.

. . . and the Sugar

• The overuse of table sugar should be discouraged along with sugary junk foods. Of course some foods, like hot cereal, may need added sugar, but in moderation. If your baby or toddler becomes accustomed to a lot of sugar, I promise you he'll always crave it.

Low-Cholesterol Diet

• Finally, I advocate feeding your children, small and large, a low-cholesterol diet. Cholesterol is a normal and vital substance in our bodies, manufactured by the body and introduced through food, but elevated levels of it (along with triglycerides) are thought to lead to the development of heart disease in susceptible people by promoting the accumulation of fat in the linings of the arteries.

Though the final proof is not yet in, I think it wise to heed the advice of most experts who assert that too much cholesterol in the diet is undesirable, especially when there is a family history of heart disease. The accumulation of fatty plaques in the arteries begins early, as proved by post-mortem examinations of American soldiers, many of them still teen-agers, in Vietnam. If your family history shows evidence of early heart disease, I suggest you have your children's cholesterol and triglyceride levels measured by your doctor. If they are found to be already high, then it is essential that their diet be changed.

It can't hurt your child to grow up on a low-cholesterol eating plan. Researchers at the University of Arizona studied a group of children reared on a "heart-healthy" diet from babyhood and found they grew as big and sturdy and healthy as those on the usual American high-fat diet.

To be considered safe, the daily diet should include no more than 300 mg of cholesterol a day. That means concentrating more on veal, poultry and fish, and cutting down on beef, fatty meats like hot dogs, sausage and bacon, pork and shellfish and especially eggs. It means substituting polyunsaturated fats for saturated fats; serving no more than three or four eggs a week; switching from whole milk to skimmed after about age six—and earlier if the child is overweight, though never before one year of age; and eliminating cream as well as cheeses made of cream.

A high-cholesterol diet, because of its high fat content, also leads to overweight. So cutting down can slim your children as well as perhaps lengthen their lives.

I will be more specific about the food your child should eat while growing up as I go along in this book. But, in general, I advocate a prudent, well-balanced diet: appropriate daily servings of the four basic food groups, low-cholesterol foods, moderate amounts of salt, decreased consumption of sugars and starches, and elimination of junk foods.

7

Scoring the Fatness Risk

Guide		Your Child
One fat parent..............	2 points	_____
Two fat parents.............	4 points	_____
Fat at 1 year	2 points	_____
Fat at 2 years..............	2 points	_____
Fat at 6 years..............	2 points	_____
Fat at 10 years.............	2 points	_____
Fat at 12 years.............	2 points	_____
Fat at 14 years.............	2 points	_____
Fat at 16–18 years	2 points	_____
	Total:	_____

At birth, the risk is

        0 points .... low

        2 points .... moderate

        4 points .... high

At 1 year:

        0–2 points .... low

        4 points .... moderate

        6 points .... high

At 2 years:

        0–2 points . . . . low

        4 points . . . . moderate

        6–8 points . . . . high

At 6 years:

        0–2 points . . . . low

        4–6 points . . . . moderate

        8–10 points . . . . high

At 10 years:

        0–4 points . . . . low

        6–8 points . . . . moderate

        10–12 points . . . . high

At 12 years:

        0–4 points . . . . low

        6–10 points . . . . moderate

        12–14 points . . . . high

At 14 years:

        0–4 points . . . . low

        6–10 points . . . . moderate

        12–16 points . . . . high

At 16–18 years:

        0–4 points . . . . low

        6–12 points . . . . moderate

        14–18 points . . . . high

If you would like to have a rough indication of your child's chances of ending up as an overweight adult, here is a guide to future fat based on my experience and common sense. Though it has not been scientifically tested, it will give an idea of what may be in store. Remember that anywhere along the line the odds for fat can change in either direction. At the beginning of each future chapter, the appropriate charts will appear so that you can score your own children's risk.

I have given point values to the most important factors related to obesity, the factors that can lead a child to a lifetime of overweight, taking into consideration the genetic aspects, the multiplication of fat cells, the patterns of eating and expenditure of energy. Crucial to this scoring system is the absolute fact that the longer a child remains fat, the greater the risk of fighting fat forever.

Statistics have shown that a child having one obese parent, and especially two obese parents, has an excellent chance of growing up fat herself. So, if one of you is persistently heavy, give your child 2 points in the box on page 65. If you are both heavy, give her 4 points.

If she is markedly fat at a year, 2 more points. And if she remains overweight at each of the ages listed in the box—2, 6, 10, 12, 14 and 16–18—give her 2 more points for each. Added up, the total number will place the child in one of three broad categories—low risk, moderate risk, or high risk.

The fewest points a child can score is obviously 0, while the most is 18. To reach 18 points, both of the parents must be obese and your sixteen- to eighteen-year-old child has been fat ever since birth. An eighteen-year-old with 18 points will, unfortunately, have little chance of ever being thin unless she remains on a perpetual restrictive regime, while another with 0 points at that age will find it almost impossible to become a fat adult. The fewer points your child accumulates, the better.

Your Child's Fatness Risk Can Change

I want to prove to you in this book that you can raise your child so that she has little chance of ending up fat. No matter how she starts off in life, she can grow up thin with a low or moderate risk for future fat. For example, even if she has two fat parents, she can be thin if her weight is carefully monitored from the moment she is born. She will end up with only 4 risk points, putting her at low risk.

On the other hand, if a child who is born to two thin parents (o points), is obese at one, two, and six, she will already have moved into the moderate-risk group and will continue into the high-risk group if she continues to be fat through the age of eighteen.

A child with one fat parent (2 points) and fat at a year (2 more points)—moderate risk—can be diverted to low risk if she is now thinned down and kept thin thereafter.

My purpose is to help you *keep* your child in the low-risk category if she is still an infant, or already older and thin; and to *switch* her to low risk, or at least moderate risk, if you have a child who is already overweight, thereby minimizing her chances of ending up fat.

Let me give you a couple of examples of children whose risk has changed. Ten-year-old John has one thin parent and one who is overweight. John was thin till the age of about one. At that time, therefore, his total score was 2 points or low risk. Then his parents were divorced and his mother began to stuff herself and the baby full of food. Now, at 10, he is decidedly fat, and his score is 8 points, almost in the high-risk category. If he continues to be overweight, he'll lose his opportunity of *ever* being a thin person.

On the other hand, little Kim was born to two fat parents (4 points). She was plump at birth and was definitely overweight at a year (6 points), which made her a high risk for future fat problems.

I discussed the situation at length with her parents, and was able to convince them of the importance of immediately starting to slow down her weight gain. Luckily, it worked. By the age of two, Kim was normal weight for her height and build, though, with 6 points, she was still technically in the high-risk group. However, when she started school at six, she was still thin, had only her original 6 points, and so had moved down to moderate risk. If she keeps up the good work, she won't have to be a fat adult.

As you read, fill in the risk-scoring boxes at the beginning of the appropriate age-group chapters, and total up the points. In what category does your child fit? Low risk? Moderate risk? High risk? If she is at low risk, you're doing a fine job. If she is at moderate or high risk, you had better get busy with the job of fatproofing. The sooner you start the better. But whenever you start, you can still improve your child's chances for a slim, happy future.

8

Your Child's Weight from Birth to One Year

Scoring the Risk at Birth

One fat parent .... 2 points
Two fat parents .... 4 points

Your baby's total .... ————

0 points makes your infant a low risk for
    future fat.
2 points makes him a moderate risk.
4 points makes him a high risk.

Scoring the Risk at 1 Year

One fat parent .... 2 points
Two fat parents .... 4 points
Fat at 1 year .... 2 points

Your baby's total .... ————

0 points means your baby is a low risk for
    future fat.
4 points means he is a moderate risk.
6 points means he is a high risk.

Most mothers of infants, I've found in my twenty years' practice as a pediatrician, are obsessed by their babies' weight. "How much did he gain this month, Doctor?" is the anxious question I hear more than any other, and I hear it every single day of the week. (The next most popular subject is bowel movements!)

If the baby has gained a lot, his mother is proud and happy. If he hasn't, she is miserable and thinks she has hopelessly failed as a mother. And nothing is more crushing to her than to discover another baby of the same age who weighs more than hers. She compares weights not only with her friends but even with complete strangers pushing their carriages in the park.

Not only mothers—and fathers, of course—are caught up with the idea that "a nice fat little baby" is the kind that's best. Everyone else—friends and relations and especially grandparents—thinks the same. Everyone loves those soft rolls of fat on a baby's tiny legs, thinks it's adorable that his neck is barely visible under his fat little chin.

Not only that, but everyone thinks a fat baby is the healthiest baby.

"What a Lovely Thin Baby!"

In truth, though nobody says, "What a lovely *thin* baby!" the thin baby is actually the healthiest baby, the baby parents should strive for. When a mother brings her infant to my office and is exceedingly proud because her two-month-old has gained three pounds that month, I am not happy. I am very upset. That infant is gaining too rapidly and is on its way to obesity.

I'll never forget Mrs. C., who came to my office with her four-month-old daughter. The baby was considerably overweight, but before I had a chance to discuss the dangers of fat with her mother, she complained, "I don't know what I'm doing wrong, but my next-door neighbor has a baby a month younger than Jennifer and she weighs a whole pound more."

I explained that the baby next door was obviously much too fat and, rather than being envious, Mrs. C. should be happy Jennifer weighed less. "In fact," I added, "what we're going to try to do is slim her down." Mrs. C. couldn't believe her ears.

When a baby is too fat, there has to be a process of *un*learning. The mother, and any others who take part in feeding the infant, have to realize that this baby must not continue to gain so rapidly. If he does, he will almost certainly become a fat two-year-old, a fat five-year-old, a fat adolescent, and eventually a fat adult. He should have all the nutrition he needs, but in the proper quantities with no excess calories which, when not burned up, will become excessive fat tissue.

Obviously, I am not advocating an emaciated baby, but a baby who is probably considered underweight by most people today—a *thin baby!*

From a short-range point of view, there is some evidence that the markedly fat baby gets sick more often than a thin one, with a higher incidence of respiratory illness. This has not yet been scientifically proved, but it's been my experience, and that of other pediatricians, and I believe it to be true.

Fat Forever?

And from the long-range point of view, the most important reason to keep an infant from becoming fat is the close association between the fat baby and the fat adult. British studies, in fact, have shown that when a baby, even as young as six weeks, has had an unusually rapid weight gain, his chance of being obese later in life is far greater than normal. If he's fat on his first birthday, his chances are even greater that he will always find it difficult to keep his weight under control as he grows older.

Along with early adolescence, the years between birth and two (and especially the first year) are the critical years when a child's fat cells increase in number the most (see Chapter 3). Once they've increased, even stringent dieting won't get rid of them. They may decrease in size but they are there forever. The process is irreversible. So, your little baby, if he's allowed to be fat, will probably have to fight for the rest of his life against the tendency to be overweight and will suffer the medical and social consequences of being fat. As I've said earlier and will stress throughout this book: Losing weight at any age is hard; preventing obesity from the beginning of life is easier and much more sensible.

The Normal Weight Gain

How much should a normal baby weigh? Of course, the numbers differ from baby to baby, depending on an infant's birth weight and body structure, but a good general rule is that a baby is doing fine if he doubles his birth weight by five months and triples it in a year. So, a six-pound baby should weigh about twelve pounds at five months and around eighteen pounds at a year. If he weighs twenty-five pounds, he's too fat.

Here, to help you get an idea of how much your infant should weigh, are the average normal weights for babies of three different birth weights at several ages up to a year.

AVERAGE NORMAL WEIGHTS

Birth Weight:	6½ lbs	7½ lbs	9 lbs
Three months:	10½ lbs	12½ lbs	14½ lbs
Six months:	14 lbs	16½ lbs	19 lbs
Nine months:	16½ lbs	20 lbs	23 lbs
One year:	18½ lbs	22 lbs	25½ lbs

Put another way, a baby is being fed enough if he gains less than two pounds a month, or half a pound a week, during his first six months. More is too fast. In the baby's second six months, his weight gain should slow down to about a pound a month. More is too much. And, obviously, if he's gaining too much, he's getting too much to eat. By the way, there's no such thing, for a healthy baby, as gaining weight too slowly.

The best way to tell if your baby is too fat, as I noted earlier, is to use the eyeball test—you can *see* when he's too chubby. I suggest, however, that you do not take the responsibility yourself of deciding whether the baby is gaining too much too fast, but rather that you be sure to take him to his doctor for regular checkups. Discuss the weight with him (her) and get his (her) help in working out a feeding plan. I recommend having no scales in the house but rather to take the baby to the doctor for weighing. Mothers who weigh their babies every day unfailingly do it to be sure they're gaining enough and have an overinvolvement with weight gain.

In my practice I have found that *most* babies gain too rapidly and tend to be too fat. And, according to Dr. Sherrel L. Hammar, assistant professor of pediatrics at the University of Hawaii, infants are doubling their birth weights at a significantly earlier age than they did several decades ago. Dr. Hammar feels this rate of gain is much too rapid—

"Maximum growth of an infant is not synonymous with optimum growth." And I agree with this completely.

Thin Parents Are Best

If you want your baby to grow up thin and healthy, the best time to start doing something about it is *before* you become pregnant. Statistically, the baby born to one fat parent has a 50 percent chance of becoming obese, and the baby born to two fat parents has an 80 percent chance of growing up fat. Obviously, the genes have something to do with this, but also important is the weight of the mother during pregnancy along with the environment of the household. Use the risk-scoring box on the first page of this chapter to get an indication of your baby's current chances of growing up overweight.

So the first step in becoming a good mother is to slim yourself down before you conceive. If you are very overweight during pregnancy, your baby can be adversely affected. Chances are he will be an oversized baby and so may cause problems in delivery. And, says obstetrician Dr. Paul L. Juan, assistant attending physician in the Department of Obstetrics and Gynecology at St. Vincent's Hospital and Medical Center in New York, the infant mortality rate among obese mothers is four times higher than among normal-weight women. Chances are, too, if the baby is large at birth, he will have more tendency to become fat later on, probably because he will be born with more than the normal number of fat cells. According to research, the last three months of pregnancy is the time when the cells first begin to multiply—and perhaps overmultiply.

A recent study in England showed that of babies who

weighed eight pounds or more at birth, 20 percent were fat at ages six to eight. Of the babies who were seven pounds or less at birth, only 7 percent were fat at ages six to eight.

The sensible thing, therefore, is to try to be within a normal weight range when you have a baby.

If, however, you are excessively overweight and have *already* become pregnant, it is important *not* to go on any crash diets. This is not the time to slim down rapidly and rashly because, if you do not have a sufficiently nutritive diet during pregnancy, the fetus may suffer from malnutrition with its many dire consequences, or from a condition called ketosis, which can be very harmful to the baby. Cut down on unnecessary calories, following a reasonable weight-control diet that includes a healthy combination of nutrients needed by you and the baby. Crash diets, if you must go on one (and I don't approve of them), must be saved till after the baby is born. If there is to be a choice, it's preferable to be heavy at delivery than to starve your unborn baby.

Feeding Your New Baby

If you really love your baby, you won't feed him too much. Most mothers think they are showing their love for their infants—and other children as well—by feeding them, and feeding them far too much. Give your baby an extra cuddle instead of an extra bottle. If you really love him, feed him only what his body requires.

Milk is the only food a baby needs for at least the first three months. It is very close to the perfect food for him. The only essential nutritive it lacks is iron, but babies are usually born with enough stored iron from the mother to last them longer than three months without requiring an additional supply from the diet. The main exception to this would be the premature baby, who often has reduced amounts of stored iron and so may need an iron-fortified formula. However, the Committee on Nutrition of the American Academy of Pediatrics recently recommended that *all* newborns be given an iron-fortified formula to minimize the risk of iron-deficiency anemia in a baby who is not fed foods containing iron. Let your pediatrician be the one to decide on the iron your infant needs.

It is a rare baby today in this country who has a vitamin deficiency. Doctors hardly ever see one outside of poverty areas. Nevertheless, I recommend that all newborns receive one of the multivitamin drops each day starting at two weeks of age.

So, for the first three months, milk, vitamins and a little water are all your new baby needs. There's no reason for solid foods; in fact, there's good reason *not* to start solids too early. Milk fills him up faster and more efficiently and without excessive calories. Babies who start solids early tend to gain weight earlier and become much too heavy by the time they are a year old.

How Much Is Enough?

Most mothers seem to be terrified that their babies will starve to death between the three o'clock feeding and the six o'clock. Most, especially mothers of firstborns, are positive their babies aren't getting enough to eat. Their chief concern is to get more food into them.

Let me assure you, as I have the parents of all my patients, that the normal baby won't starve. He'll drink as much milk as he needs, given the opportunity. The baby will stop when he is full, and you needn't worry about underfeeding him. If offered his feeding, he will take all that he requires for normal growth and development. Forget the idea that he's going to waste away by morning. Obviously, if your baby completely refuses his milk feedings or takes only a small amount compared to what he previously has been consuming, you should discuss this with your baby's doctor.

Try to remember that it doesn't matter whether your infant consumes two ounces of formula at a feeding or four ounces, or more. If he's satisfied, he's had enough. Don't push any more on him. He's satisfied when he stops pulling at the nipple. Don't worry if he doesn't finish a bottle. It means he isn't hungry right now, just as you may not be hungry occasionally. The amount of milk a baby needs and wants varies from day to day and baby to baby. It isn't a catastrophe if your infant drinks less than your best friend's. As a matter of fact, it may even be better that he does.

About how much milk should a baby take? It's been calculated that he needs about fifty calories per pound per day. Since each ounce of breast milk and prepared formula contains twenty calories, most newborns would require two and a half ounces of milk per pound per day. Obviously, the amount a baby drinks would then depend on his weight. A ten-pounder would need more milk than a five-pound baby. For example, a six-pound baby would require about fifteen ounces of milk each twenty-four hours in order to get fifty calories per pound.

Just because you know the general rule of thumb concerning the amount of milk the majority of newborns seem to need, that does not mean that you must make certain, no matter how difficult it is, that your infant drinks precisely that amount. As I've said, babies differ and there shouldn't be a contest between you and the baby to see that he conforms to any general rules. Nor with your neighbor to see who produces a fatter baby. You won't be showing your love for your baby by stuffing the milk into him because it's "good for him." In truth, it's good for him to receive only the amount of food his body needs and his appetite wants—within reason, of course. If you are uncertain, by all means consult your baby's doctor.

Breast vs. Bottle Feeding

I am always asked by expectant mothers whether I prefer breast or bottle feeding. The question is not what *I* prefer, but what the mother prefers. In the United States at the present time, one in four mothers breast-feed their babies. Put another way, three out of four babies are bottle-fed. Strictly from the nutritional point of view, both groups do equally well. With the excellent ready-to-feed, convenient, prepared formulas available today, a bottle-fed baby receives pretty much the same milk as the breast-fed baby—a beautifully balanced diet of water, sugar, protein and fat, plus minerals and vitamins.

Nevertheless, I am always very pleased when a new mother is truly anxious to breast-feed her baby and I encourage her to do so. The mother who anticipates breast feeding with joy and pleasure does beautifully because the experience can be satisfying and fulfilling. It is the most pleasant, relaxed way for both mother and baby to enjoy the feedings. The warmth and closeness of mother and baby are very important for the baby's future emotional health. All babies love to be held close and cuddled by the person doing the feeding, and breast feeding is perfect for this. Human milk is ideally suited to the baby's needs, and, in addition, there is evidence that breast milk contains antibodies that may protect the baby against certain illnesses.

Problems arise with the mother who breast-feeds for the wrong reasons. In my experience, the mother who is pressured into it by her mother-in-law or her friends or her own compulsiveness is making a mistake even to start. The mother who breast-feeds because she'll feel guilty if she doesn't does neither herself nor her baby a bit of good. It seldom works out well and in a short time her baby will undoubtedly be switched over to the bottle. I would therefore strongly recommend that you do not start to breast-feed unless you are enthusiastic about it.

There is absolutely no reason to feel guilty if you would rather not or cannot breast-feed your baby. There is nothing wrong with bottle feeding and you won't be shortchanging your infant. I remember a new mother who was terribly upset over her difficulty in breast-feeding. We talked about it for a while and I told her there was abolutely no reason for her to feel guilty—to breast-feed or not is just a matter of choice. But it came out that her mother-in-law had said to her during her pregnancy, "All my daughters breast-fed their babies and I certainly expect my son's wife will do the same." If Grandma had been there at the time, she'd have heard a few well-chosen words from me.

If your aim is to have a *thin* healthy baby, however, breast-feeding has a distinct advantage. Studies have shown that breast-fed babies end up on the average less fat than those who are bottle-fed. If you breast-feed, you won't know exactly how much milk your baby is consuming and that's a good thing. All you will know is when the baby is satisfied. The mother of a bottle-fed baby *does* know exactly how much milk he takes and usually worries if he doesn't finish his bottle and if he doesn't drink as much as *she* feels he should. She has a greater tendency to attempt to feed him every time he cries. She hears him crying, stuffs the bottle in his mouth and the baby quickly gets the idea that food is comfort and happiness. He will be overfed and overweight.

Crying May Not Mean He's Hungry

There are many reasons for a baby to cry other than hunger. After an adequate feeding, even if he hasn't completely finished his bottle, it's impossible for him to be hungry for at least three hours, the time it takes for the stomach to empty. So, if your baby is crying and it has been less than three hours since the last feeding, don't look to the bottle to hush him up. See if you can find out what really is bothering him. Maybe he has gas, maybe he's wet and doesn't like it, maybe a pin is sticking into him, or perhaps he's teething. Or maybe he's just plain cranky. There are babies who cry because they cry, and you'll never know why.

It's very hard to convince parents that crying is perfectly normal. As far as I'm concerned, a certain amount of crying is good exercise and nothing to worry about. But if you can't bear listening to it, please don't automatically assume your baby is hungry and feed him every time he cries. *He won't starve.* The misuse of the bottle starts him on the road to overweight and gives him the idea that all his problems can be solved by food. It teaches him to misread his internal cues till he won't know that eating is intended only to satisfy hunger.

What should you do instead, if you've looked for every possible cause, found none, and your baby is still crying? Offer him a little water. Pick him up, pat him, cuddle him. Perhaps he has a strong sucking need as some babies do.

Give him a pacifier which will satisfy him without giving him unnecessary calories. He'll be contented and can wait till he's really hungry before his next feeding.

Just remember to remove the pacifier when he falls asleep—it should not become a permanent fixture in his little mouth. Besides, if he becomes accustomed to the pacifier when he's sleeping, he'll wake up and complain every time it falls out, day or night.

I also suggest giving your baby a pacifier only in his first few months when the sucking drive is strong, or he may become too attached to it and find it very difficult to give up.

A Time to Relax

The secret of successful feeding, breast or bottle, is to be relaxed about the whole thing. Sit in a comfortable chair and hold the baby cuddled in your arms. Do not prop the bottle and leave the baby on his own—holding him is just as important as feeding him. Take your time—there is no hurry. Each feeding should last at least fifteen or twenty minutes, in order to satisfy both the hunger and the sucking needs of your infant. An unhurried, relaxed mealtime is the key to eating habits that will be established very early. We know that eating fast and nervously is unhealthy and leads to eating too much. Studies have found that eating more slowly can satisfy hunger needs with fewer calories than gulping the food down.

On the other hand, don't stretch the feeding time out longer than a half hour. If your baby hasn't finished his bottle in that time, all it means is that he doesn't want any more. If he is working very hard but is not getting much milk down, be sure the nipple is unclogged and has a large enough opening.

Burps Aren't All the Same

Babies need to be burped during their feedings because they swallow air as they drink, but it's hard to tell a new mother just how to do it. Some babies need to be burped every ounce or so; others refuse to burp and, if you attempt to make them do so, won't go back to sucking. They have to be burped when they're all finished. Some babies are hard to burp, and others are easy. Some prefer one position, and some another. And some, no matter what you do, won't burp until they're put down in their cribs. You'll just have to see what your baby prefers.

If the baby needs to burp and you haven't given him the chance, he'll retain the air he's swallowed and will probably become quite uncomfortable. He'll cry. Don't be fooled by the crying and give him more milk; that will only aggravate the situation. Help him to burp; remember what I've just pointed out—that all crying doesn't come from hunger.

Some babies have a natural tendency to drink very fast, too fast. In that case, modify the bottle nipple so it doesn't release so much milk so quickly. Getting the milk should require work, in the form of hard sucking.

Some babies, even on an exclusive milk diet, may gain weight at too rapid a rate. Although it's impossible here to individualize for each baby, keep in mind that a gain that more than doubles the birth weight at five months or triples it in a year, and a monthly weight gain of over two pounds, would be considered excessive for any baby.

Cut Down the Calories

If your baby is gaining too rapidly—and your doctor is the one to tell you if he is—my best advice would be simply to dilute the whole milk in his bottle with water. If, for example, he takes six ounces at a feeding, drop the milk content of the bottle to four ounces and add two ounces of water. This will reduce the number of calories but not the volume, and will give him more than enough nutrition. I've found this an effective way to allow a baby to gain at a normal rate. I don't recommend using skimmed milk before at least one year of age because it is not yet known whether it is the proper food for an infant. According to Dr. Samuel J. Fomon, consultant in nutrition to the federal Maternal and Child Care Service, the use of skimmed milk in infancy may give an undesirably high intake of protein and an undesirably low intake of fat. Of course, in the case of a breast-fed baby, diluting the milk is impossible, but, as I've said, these babies tend not to be overweight anyway.

Feeding Schedules

How often should you feed your new baby? I suppose the best answer I could give is to feed him as often as is necessary to satisfy the hunger drive, and this obviously varies from baby to baby. I do not believe in a rigid schedule, but rather a modified demand schedule, which you and the baby can work out. I do advise that you do not feed your baby more often than every three hours. After an adequate feeding, even if he hasn't finished the bottle, he will not be hungry for at least three hours because, as I've said previously, it takes that long for his stomach to empty. So, if the baby is fussy and crying less than three hours after the feeding, you'll know it's not from hunger. After a while, you will probably learn to differentiate between hunger crying, discomfort crying, and plain ordinary fussy crying.

If the baby sleeps more than five hours at a stretch during the day, it's sensible to wake him up and feed him. That's so he'll eventually learn to do his big sleeping at night and his eating in the daytime. Never wake him during the night, though, no matter how long he sleeps. If he is sleeping, he can't be hungry, so why feed him? One exception: if your baby always wakes up hungry, say, at 2:00 or 3:00 A.M., it is a good idea to wake him to offer a bottle at around 11:00 P.M., just before you go to bed, in the hope that it will hold him till the next morning. This may or may not work, but it's worth a try.

Starting Solid Foods

Some mothers just can't wait for the day to come when they can begin to spoon-feed their infants. They feel their baby isn't getting enough nourishment from milk alone, that solid food will fill him up more and make him content and healthy. This anxiety, for some reason, is especially true of bottle mothers. Breast-feeding mothers usually are less frantic about the introduction of solid foods.

The fact is, the only food that babies should be fed for the first few months—at least three, though they could go much longer than that—is milk and vitamins. There is absolutely no reason for solids before then, and I spend a lot of time and effort trying to convince my mothers of that. Their babies are getting all the nourishment they need without a spoonful of solid food.

Aside from that, there is reason to believe that beginning solids too early tends to lead to overly fat babies and overly fat children who will always have a weight problem. Babies who are started on solids very early are heavier by age one than those who are started later. If our goal is to have *thin* healthy babies, then it's important to wait until the babies *need* the additional foods.

In October 1974, a research study of a group of randomly

selected well infants by faculty members of the Johns Hopkins School of Hygiene and Public Health revealed that 97 percent of the infants were already being fed cereal at two months, and 70 percent were dining on strained fruit. One out of five of the infants was given solid food before a week of age.

The research team also found that the protein intake of the babies was almost 60 percent above recommended dietary allowance, and calorie intake was 30 percent too high.

Said Dr. David M. Paige, a pediatrician and one of the authors of the study, at a meeting of the American Public Health Association, "It is important that mothers do not yield to the strong commercial and peer pressures to introduce baby foods too soon. Milk foods alone provide adequate nutrition for most babies for the first six months of life."

Mothers obviously feel that their babies *need* baby food along with milk just as early as possible, that they are being "good mothers" if they offer it. Obviously that is not true. "Good mothers," once they know the facts, will hold back until the proper time.

One new mother called me when her baby was ten days old. She said her infant, who had been seven pounds two ounces when he went home from the hospital, had gained ten ounces in those five days and "is always hungry. Couldn't I give him some cereal to help fill him up?" Her mother had made the suggestion. It was obvious the baby couldn't possibly have been hungry; he was already gaining much too fast, twice as fast as the average weight gain of one ounce a day. I advised her that she was overfeeding him and to dilute the formula with water. He was much too young for her to think about feeding him solids.

However, when she brought her baby in for his first monthly checkup, he had gained a total of three pounds. He was definitely fat, and the mother couldn't have been prouder of her accomplishments. She told me she hadn't taken my advice but had started him on a little cereal and fruit when he was two weeks old. She said he got angry when he didn't get enough to eat. I told her *I* was angry, that she was obviously planning to raise a fat child who was going to have all the problems she, who was quite definitely far overweight, must have had. I tried to convince her that fat did not lead to health and happiness. She managed to hold back a little, but when I saw the baby recently at eighteen months, he was still definitely a fatty.

The reason I advise mothers not to feed their babies solids too early, aside from the fact that they don't need them nutritionally, is that solids are high-density calorie foods, while milk is of lower density. In other words, a baby can drink milk and have his hunger satisfied with fewer calories than by solid foods. He is filled up faster on milk. It requires more solid food, and therefore more calories, to satisfy a baby on solids. Put another way, if you fill a baby up to the point of satisfaction with solids, you have to give him more calories to do it than you do using milk. So, by holding back on the solid foods for *at least* the first three months, you can cut down his weight gain while keeping him perfectly happy and healthy.

Solids at Three Months or So

At about three months or later, I advise starting your baby on a little precooked cereal. Since cereals are iron-fortified, this is a nice way to introduce iron into the diet. The portions should be *very* small, perhaps a tablespoon or two, mixed with milk or formula, twice a day. It usually takes a few days of practice for a baby to learn to swallow from a spoon, so be patient.

I advise against putting solid food into the bottle. If you do, your baby, who previously took his milk with no fuss, may decide to refuse it now and you'll have a real problem. My feeling is that solids should be given only by spoon. If your baby rejects the food, don't worry about it. Wait a few days and try again, but don't be insistent. It doesn't matter if he takes only milk for a while longer.

Try to get away without adding any sugar to the cereal. Mothers sprinkle it on because *they* think it tastes better that way, but many babies will take it as is. The less sugar your baby takes in, the better off he will be. He'll stay slimmer, your dental bills will be lower, and he won't be so likely to turn into a Milky Way addict later on. Some babies won't eat cereal without sugar, but use the least amount he'll accept. Some mothers like to add sugar to their baby's drinking water, too. I advise against it unless the baby absolutely refuses the water without it. Then add only a *little* sugar. Moderation is the key word. Patterns of eating are established very early and you must never forget this.

Once the baby has become accustomed to the cereal, I suggest starting him on small amounts of strained fruits twice a day, then strained vegetables at lunch. At four to five months, strained meats can be introduced at lunch. And strained egg yolks for breakfast at about six months (no more than three or four a week).

It's wise not only to stay away from too much sugar, but also too much salt. Often, when a baby doesn't eat a food, his mother will sprinkle salt on it to improve its taste. I don't encourage this, with a few exceptions. Eggs, for example, do seem to require a little salt. But the salt used in normal cooking is sufficient, and certainly the most popular prepared baby foods don't need more than they already contain. Many not only have too many calories but a much too high salt content. A child who becomes accustomed to a lot of salt may well develop high blood pressure later in his life.

Every new food should be started by giving the baby just one teaspoon the first day and gradually increasing each day. Wait at least three days between new foods to be certain your baby tolerates what he's given. The signs of food intolerance include vomiting, rashes, gassiness, and excessive crankiness. If the baby reacts adversely to any of the foods he's given, stop giving them to him and ask your doctor which substitutes to make.

No need to measure out portions exactly. You can't know exactly how much the baby will want at a particular meal. Just provide enough to feed him as much as he wants without any coaxing from you. Keep calm. Remember what I've been telling you—that in my experience practically all parents think their baby should eat much more than he needs to eat.

While I don't advocate starting solids too early, I do recommend that they are begun by around four months. This is because the baby will by now have pretty well used up his natural store of iron and will need some from his diet. He'll get it from the iron-fortified cereals and from green vegetables, meats, and egg yolks. If he remains on milk alone for the first nine to twelve months, he will certainly become anemic. The rare baby who refuses solid food should be given iron supplements starting at four months.

After the baby is six months old, "baby dinners" and teething crackers and single desserts may be added, usually followed by junior and table foods. This is about the right time to start offering your baby sips of water or juice from a cup; it will prepare him for weaning later on. I see no necessity to start orange juice until the baby is six or seven months old. Most infants just don't like the taste and it may also cause them to develop rashes or spit up. Besides, they don't require orange juice since they get all the Vitamin C they need in their daily multivitamin drops.

Healthy Finger Foods

Now you can also give the baby "finger foods" like zweiback teething biscuits, toast, and bits of banana—he'll manage to get some of it into his mouth and he'll love being a do-it-yourselfer. By nine months, he'll probably be able to handle pieces of cheese, slices of apple, and well-done scrambled eggs. Finger foods at this age will give him practice for spoon-feeding himself later on when he's about a year old. You'll notice that I did not include cookies and cake and candy and pretzels, etc., in my suggested finger foods. Certainly a cookie now and then won't hurt, but a cookie all the time will. It will help make your baby fat. There's no need to make him overly fond of sweets at this age, or any age for that matter. He'll be perfectly happy with *nourishing* snacks.

Just recently a mother came in to see me with a very heavy eight-month-old. Just as I was about to chastise her for letting the baby get too fat, she said, "Dr. Eden, what am I going to do? This baby refuses to eat. If I get three teaspoons of meat in her mouth at dinner, I'm lucky."

We carefully calculated just what the baby actually did eat in twenty-four hours and it turned out that she *didn't* eat much at meals. What was creating the problem was the tremendous amount of *between-meal* "nourishment" she consumed. Her mother was so concerned that she get enough food that she stuffed her with juice and cookies, crackers and ice cream. No wonder she wasn't hungry for dinner.

Among the questions I'm always asked by mothers is, "Should I give my baby his milk or his solid food first?"

Some babies refuse any solid food after taking their milk and so should, of course, be given their food first. Other babies have no preference, take whatever is given first, and are hungry enough for both. A method that I've found effective for many babies is to start the meal by giving part of the bottle; then follow with the solid foods; and finish off with the rest of the bottle.

How Much Milk?

Some babies, even after they've started on solids, take a tremendous amount of milk. I recommend not giving your baby more than a quart a day, so there will be some room left for solid food. If he drinks more than that, he'll obviously be so full he won't feel like eating. In any case, a quart is more than enough—a baby needs considerably less to get all the nourishment he needs.

During the first six or seven months, a baby's appetite for solid food is usually minimal. He doesn't want, and he doesn't require, very much. So, if he doesn't take much, don't worry! It's perfectly all right. In fact, it's good. Feed him as much milk and/or food as he'll happily take in a reasonable period of time. Then put the food away and wait for the next meal and do the same. Later, often toward the end of the baby's first year, when he increases his activity—pulling himself up and crawling—his appetite will be much larger.

A Half Hour Per Feeding

A relatively *short* time should be spent feeding your baby after he graduates to solid foods. I'd say half an hour for both milk and solids is the absolute maximum and that's stretching it. It's plenty of time for him to have taken as much as he needs. I've heard stories from mothers who've spent an hour or an hour and a half trying to stuff strained vegetables into their babies. Both mother and child have to end up feeling irritable.

I remember a mother who came into the office looking exhausted, as though she hadn't slept in weeks. She hadn't. The reason was that she spent a minimum of two hours at each feeding of her firstborn infant, so that one feeding literally ran into the next. This went on from 6:00 A.M. till midnight; then the baby slept until six.

I said, "Well, then you get at least six hours sleep."

"No," she said, "that's when I do my housework."

At six months, this same baby had more than tripled his birth weight. Born seven pounds, he was now twenty-two pounds and rolling in fat. There was no question that the baby already had a tremendous increase in his number of fat cells and was well on his way to becoming a fat person. The mother told me that he was always crying for more food.

I think I was able to reverse the trend, and convinced both the mother and father, who were considerably over-weight themselves, how important it was that the baby not gain weight so rapidly. I told them that a half hour was plenty of time to spend feeding him and that he was probably crying from gassiness because of overeating. He was no doubt swallowing too much air. The baby, now two years old, is not what you would call thin, but he is almost within the range of normal weight for his height. Besides, everybody in the house is now sleeping through the night.

Some mothers call me frantically to tell me their babies haven't eaten a thing all day. What should they do? I reassure them that there's nothing to worry about—some milk and vitamins are all the baby really needs that day.

Let the Baby Decide How Much He Wants

The normal healthy growing baby, like the newborn infant, knows how much he wants to eat, and you must not force him to eat the amount *you* decide he wants. His appetite should determine how much he gets, and it will vary from day to day. There's no law that says he must finish his bottle or his plate. The earlier a parent learns this, the better off the baby will be. I do recommend regular, periodic visits to the pediatrician, where the baby will be weighed and measured and examined. If he's growing and developing and gaining at a normal rate *as determined by the doctor,* and not by you or your husband or your mother-in-law, he is doing just fine, no matter how much or how little he eats. Let him eat what he feels like eating.

I had a call one night at 2:00 A.M. from a frantic mother. Her five-month-old baby had eaten only two tablespoons of squash instead of his usual four tablespoons! I couldn't believe that she was calling me at that hour for such a reason and I never did discover why she was feeding the baby squash then. But I remember telling her that worrying about each tablespoon was not only unnecessary, it was idiotic. And I requested that in the future she call to ask advice at a different hour.

It's seldom necessary to coax a growing baby to eat, and it's *never* necessary to force him. Mealtime should not be a contest between mother and baby. If you make your baby eat more than his appetite demands, you'll make him anxious and you'll make him fat. You'll make him associate eating with making you happy, certainly an inappropriate reason to eat. The end of a meal should come when he's had enough, and not when *you* think he's had enough.

One mother recently brought her seven-month-old baby to my office for her monthly checkup and was inordinately pleased when the nurse weighed the baby who had gained three pounds in the past month. This was a huge weight gain and much too much. The mother was very proud that she'd been able to stuff tremendous amounts of "very healthy" food into her baby by distracting her. She played music during the meals, sang songs, and ran around and around the child, getting her so excited and agitated by the carrying on that the baby ate everything her mother pushed into her.

I told the mother to turn off the record player, keep her own mouth shut, and to feed her baby only as much as the child wanted. I also explained to her that, although she meant well by trying so hard, all she was doing was creating problems for her child later on. The amount of food she managed to get into the baby by standing on her head would do harm in the long run.

"Be a Good Boy and Eat."

Very early, babies begin to recognize their mother's intense interest in what they eat. They begin to realize that eating up brings them approval—"What a good boy! He finished his whole supper!" Mother's happy when Baby eats. Mother's unhappy, angry, sad when Baby doesn't.

She should not worry about how much or how little food is eaten, because, as long as the baby is offered milk and the right kind of foods, he'll be nutritionally healthy. If he eats less than many mothers would like, he'll be building up lean body mass and keeping the fat tissue down to a minimum. He'll be healthier than the fat baby in every way.

It's inappropriate for a baby to eat to please his mother, to eat because she is singing and dancing or angry and scowling. It's appropriate for him to eat because he's hungry and to eat only enough to satisfy that hunger in a neutral atmosphere. If he finishes his bottle and his food, the reaction should be no different than if he leaves half of everything. Nature has a marvelous way of regulating the amount of food and calories consumed with the normal appetite mechanism. Experiments have shown that if a child is offered various kinds of food as frequently as he wants (*before* he's been taught to prefer sweets), he will take in a well-balanced and sufficient diet entirely on his own.

So, don't be frantic when your baby eats. Try not to show that you even notice the amount he does or does not consume. He shouldn't have to worry about how much he eats. All that should be required is that he is offered the right food. If he eats, fine. If he doesn't, just as fine. Now, at this early age, is the time when permanent eating patterns are starting to be established. What you do now, therefore, will affect your child's future.

Baby's Food Preferences

"My baby doesn't like some of the foods I give him. In fact, he'll only eat a few things. What should I do?" That's a question I hear very frequently. Mothers worry if their babies won't eat lots of different foods.

My answer is, don't do anything. Offer your child the foods, but don't insist that he eat a wide variety. You're not a bad mother because your baby doesn't eat string beans or chicken. Babies have food preferences, just as adults do. They don't need great variety to do well. They don't need *any* variety if it comes to that, though certainly it should be offered regularly. As long as they get *some* food that contains iron (iron-fortified cereals, green vegetables, meat, or egg yolk), they'll do fine because everything else they require is in the milk.

As the baby approaches the age of a year, his appetite

normally increases till he eats a considerable quantity of solid food every day. Now he's much more active than before—creeping, pulling himself up, moving around. The first year is a period of fantastically rapid growth, with an average height increase of ten inches and an average weight gain of fifteen pounds from birth (or triple his birth weight). The baby's appetite usually matches this growth, making the traditionally food-oriented mother deliriously happy. Now, she doesn't have to *push* milk and solids on the baby—he *wants* them! At this age, too, he is beginning to understand, and to start trying to please. Let him please you with his behavior, his good nature—*don't* make him do it with his food.

If Your Baby Is Overweight

If your baby's weight gain exceeds the normal for his height, your job now is to slow it down. You don't want him to lose weight but merely to decelerate the gain. It's easy to accomplish that goal because, at this age, you (or your substitute) control everything your baby eats. He's not yet old enough to raid the cookie jar (which I hope you don't have in your house anyway), though he is old enough to know how much he wants to eat. If he's gaining .too rapidly, dilute his milk as I've described (but don't give him skimmed milk yet), stay away from starchy and sugary foods. If he's hungry, he won't refuse the nutritious foods you offer him. Since he eats only what you give him, it's quite simple now to cut down on his calories, even if he has developed a voracious appetite.

Even Babies Need Regular Exercise

Even at this age, before your baby is a year old, he needs to get regular exercise. He wants to crawl and turn over, sit up, and eventually stand.

Babies thrive on having their extremities moved and pulling themselves up on your fingers, even being walked. They enjoy gentle stimulation and they get great pleasure from the activity.

Besides, exercise helps them burn up calories, tone up their muscles and make them strong. And it will help establish whether they're active or sedentary later on, an enormous influence on their eventual weight.

I don't think I need to qualify all this with a caution, but I will: *everything in moderation.* Don't be excessively rough with a baby and don't get him wildly overexcited anytime but especially after meals or before bedtime. He needs to have fun and exercise, but he doesn't need hysterics.

To get an idea of what your baby's chances are of one day becoming a fat-battling adult, check his risk score in the box provided at the beginning of this chapter. If he was a big baby at birth and he is overweight at a year (especially if one or both parents are fat), he's already becoming a high risk for a fat future. You can reverse the trend by slowing his weight gain.

If he's thin now, be sure he doesn't become too fat as time goes on, or your low-risk baby may move up to the moderate- or high-risk categories.

9

One- to Two-Year-Olds:
The Crucial Age for Staying Thin

Scoring the Risk at 1 Year

One fat parent .... 2 points
Two fat parents .... 4 points
Fat at 1 year .... 2 points

Your baby's total .... ————

0 points means your baby is a low risk for
    future fat.
4 points means she is a moderate risk.
6 points means she is a high risk.

Scoring the Risk at 2 Years

One fat parent .... 2 points
Two fat parents .... 4 points
Fat at 1 year .... 2 points
Fat at 2 years .... 2 points

Your child's total .... ————

0–2 points means your child has a low risk of
    future fat.
4 points means she has a moderate risk.
6–8 points means she has a high risk.

By the time your year-old baby is two, she will have established eating patterns that will remain with her for the rest of her life. That's why it's so important that you feed her the right way *now,* long before she's two. If she's going to grow up thin and healthy, she must be thin *now.* This period is most important in preventing your child from ending up as a fat adult. The fat-cell studies have discovered that some fat two-year-olds have as many fat cells as, or more than, some adults. If that's true of your baby, she'll spend her life fighting the pounds. The number of her fat cells will never decrease and they'll always be more than eager to sop up fat.

If, on the other hand, you keep your baby's weight down during her first two years, you'll go a long way toward having her grow up thin. Half the battle will be over. Be especially concerned if one of you, the mother or the father, is overweight, and even more concerned if you are both fat. Not only is there a genetic component to obesity, but babies learn from example. If you are overweight, your child may have a tendency to be heavy also.

So, this—from ages one to two—is a most crucial time in your baby's life, a time when she develops fat cells and eating habits. Because she's becoming verbal and can make her wishes quite clear, she will become involved in deciding what kind of food and how much of it she gets. She'll learn to ask for what she wants and turn down what she doesn't. She can even begin to feed herself now, making it easier for you not to overfeed her because she'll want to stop eating when she's full.

It's a crucial time, and an excellent time to establish proper eating patterns. Normally the baby's appetite begins to decrease now because her rate of growth and gain slows down to half the pace of the first year of life. A baby's average weight gain in the second year is five to six pounds, as compared to fifteen in the first year. The average height increase is five inches rather than the previous ten. She won't triple her weight again—if she did, a seven-pound newborn who is twenty-one pounds at a year would weigh sixty-three pounds at two, a record for a two-year-old.

Those "Picky" Eaters

Mothers often become terribly concerned when their baby's appetite drops off. "She used to eat so well, Doctor, but now she's so picky. She hardly eats anything. She's bigger—she should eat more." They become panicked and do everything but stand on their heads (and I know one mother who actually did *that!*) to get the food in. I as a pediatrician have to convince them that their child isn't *supposed* to eat so much now. Her appetite decrease is *normal,* and the next time she'll eat as heartily as she did before will not be until early adolescence, her next rapid growth period. Her appetite coincides with growth and so she requires less food.

Some mothers refuse to believe this, because, to them, feeding their children is their way of showing their love and of making certain they will be sturdy and healthy. "Eat, eat, my child!" is their constant cry. They feel guilty, think they are not "good mothers," if their babies don't consume a lot of food. If you are this kind of mother, try to find other ways to show your love—substitute a hug for food. Your baby will be much better for it. Don't feel guilty—she'll have much less chance to be fat and miserable later on. You can show your love by keeping her healthy and thin.

Because she's not so hungry now, use this opportunity to offer her only the foods her body needs. Avoid the sweets and put your emphasis on high-quality food. That means adequate amounts of the foods in the four basic food groups (see Chapter 6 on Nutrition). Your baby needs all of them in proper proportion.

The typical American diet consists of much too high a proportion of carbohydrates and fats. Generally short-changed are fruits and vegetables which your baby (and everyone) needs plenty of. If she learns to love them now, when she is so small, she'll always love them—and she'll continue to eat a more balanced and healthy diet than the rest of us.

A typical daily menu for an eighteen-month-old child might be: Breakfast—juice, cereal, an egg (three or four times a week), milk. Lunch—meat, vegetable, fruit, potatoes or pasta or bread. Dinner—fish, cheese, salad, fruit.

I suggest multivitamin drops daily as well.

No Force-Feeding

I am not talking about *amounts* of food, the size of the portions, because these should be decided by the child. Offer a reasonable amount of food, in a pleasant environment, try to make it look tempting, and that's all. If the baby eats not a spoonful, it simply means she's not hungry. Take it away with no comments or tension or facial expressions. Be neutral about it. If she only eats some, do the same. If she eats it all up and wants more, give it to her, again with no delighted expression or "What a good girl! You're eating such a good dinner!" Restrain yourself from, "I'm so proud you ate all your vegetables." It's *her* business!

I know it is hard to take this casual attitude—after all, you may have gone to a lot of work preparing the food, you were brought up to clean your plate, and you want your baby to be healthy. But now we know that it's not healthy to be fat, that it's important to be thin—even, and especially, at this early age.

It's better to offer your baby small portions and have her ask for more than to give her unrealistically large amounts that she can't finish. I don't think I've ever seen a mother offer her baby too small a portion, or seldom even a moderate portion. It's usually so large the child can't finish it comfortably.

If you can give her enormous portions and then not be upset when she doesn't finish it all up, fine, but most mothers can't manage that. They're disturbed by food left over on the plate. The baby recognizes that. She understands when her mother is happy and when she is angry or distressed, and, because children basically like to please their parents, she will tend to try to eat more. If she eats beyond what her appetite dictates, she is eating too much. You'll never know how much you "should" feed her—that's why it's pointless to measure out portions. If you allow *her* to decide how much food she needs, you'll never go wrong.

As for milk, that depends on your one- to two-year-old baby's feeling about it. Some don't care for it, others drink large quantities. The minimum daily amount at this stage should be two glasses a day—that is plenty for nutritional purposes. The maximum should be no more than a quart a day. If you find your baby isn't at all interested in her solid food, perhaps she is filling up too much on milk. Let her eat first, then give her her milk.

A Low-Cholesterol Diet

Make a point not to give your baby red meat all the time; in fact, I'd suggest keeping it down to about twice or three times a week. Poultry, veal and fish not only contain less fat but also less cholesterol. Though veal is expensive, chicken and turkey and some kinds of fish are not.

Fish is an especially healthful food—high protein and low fat—and should be encouraged for all of us, not only babies. Get your baby used to eating it at least two times a week;

she'll like it if she's introduced to it early. Many adults do not care for fish because they were not accustomed to eating it as children, and so they don't prepare it for their children either. Most babies love tuna fish and broiled fish of all kinds—without bones, of course.

Give your child eggs, an excellent source of protein, but keep them to a maximum of three or four a week as their cholesterol content is high.

And keep in mind my previous advice about sugar and salt. Babies often like their food just as well without sweetening or with just a little bit. Don't get them used to excessive amounts of sugar; if you do, they'll always want it. They not only don't need it but it can do them harm eventually.

The same applies to salt. Keep the salt down to a minimum because people who become accustomed to large amounts of it have a distinct tendency to develop high blood pressure later in life.

What About Variety?

Mothers frequently feel that if they don't introduce a variety of foods early, the baby will not take to new foods later. Not true. And while it's certainly nice if your baby eats a wide variety of nutritious foods, it's not a matter of life or death that she does. Some of the healthiest patients I have live almost entirely on hamburger. Others eat only chicken. If your toddler insists on eating only a few foods, that's enough, as long as she gets her milk and vitamins. Often mothers tell me that their child will only eat hot dogs, and no other meat. I say, then feed her hot dogs. They're not as nutritious as other meats but they do have some protein, and maybe you can get a little fish into her too. Keep offering other foods but don't insist.

I'm often told, too, that some babies don't like vegetables. It's rare that a baby refuses every single vegetable; usually one or two at least will appeal to her. But even if she eats no vegetables at all, she'll get along. She can live without vegetables. Take the pressure off by giving her her vitamins every day. That way you won't have to concern yourself with whether she's getting enough vitamins in her diet. Of course, it makes good sense to offer her a vegetable regularly, just in case you'll eventually hit on one she likes. One toddler I know has discovered artichokes and loves them. Children usually do acquire the taste for vegetables if they're offered them early, without fuss and without undue pressure. Cooked vegetables, however, are often a big hangup for children, and many do better with raw vegetables. If your baby likes them raw, that's fine. Nutritionally, in fact, it's usually better. It's perfectly OK never to eat a cooked vegetable.

From my point of view, if a child eats just one kind of fruit and one vegetable, cooked or raw, one kind of meat or fish, and not much of any of them, it's just as healthy for the moment as eating every food you can dream of. You may get tired of putting the same food on the table every day, and it's reasonable to ask the child to try a little of this and that, but don't make a federal case out of it. Don't make it a contest between you and the baby to be sure she gets what *you* decide she must have. It's *her* stomach. You *can* make an attempt to push the *good* food, merely by offering it, food such as yellow and green vegetables, chicken or fish, fruit, etc. Chicken is better for the baby than hot dogs, but hot dogs are better than nothing.

"Doctor, She Won't Eat!"

Suppose your baby refuses her meat, or her vegetables, or her fruit for a few days? Don't panic. It's no catastrophe.

Even if she takes very little or eats only in spurts that differ from day to day, she'll be 100 percent better off than the child whose food is shoved down her throat. Nothing terrible will happen even if the baby completely skips a meal. She won't waste away between lunch and dinner. She won't develop a vitamin defficiency or malnutrition, nor will she be particularly susceptible to infection, something mothers always worry about. She'll eat tomorrow or the next day when she's hungry.

No matter how difficult it is for you if your baby doesn't feel like eating much, or anything at all, at this meal, don't struggle with her. Walk away from it. As far as that baby is concerned, you're not bothered at all. Take my word for it—she won't starve to death (you'd be amazed how many mothers are really convinced that could happen), and she won't get the idea that food is the most important thing in the world. You might perhaps offer her the same meal a half hour or an hour later, or give her her next meal a little early, but please don't try to tide her over with cookies. Then she certainly won't be hungry next time around. When she *is* hungry, she'll take the good nutritious food you give her.

I don't think it's at all wise to let your baby become accustomed to rich desserts after her meals. There's no law that says we must always end a meal with something fattening and sweet; that's one of those American eating habits that has helped lead us to become a generation of fat people. Instead of pudding or cake, give your child fruit or cheese, or nothing at all. Many babies become accustomed to even the "strange" tasting cheeses.

No Bribery

Above all, please don't give your child a sweet dessert, or anything else, as a bribe or a reward for eating up her vegetables. That's using food for the wrong reasons. If she finishes her dinner because you've said, "Lisa, if you eat the very last spoonful of everything, you know what? I'm going to give you some chocolate pudding!" she'll both be eating more than she wants and learning that sweets are to be coveted. She equates finishing all the food with the contentment she feels from her mother's approval. And she equates it with pudding and cake. Food should be used for satisfying hunger. Period. I strongly object to the bribery and reward system. It can be the beginning of the obesity problem.

Certainly, if your baby is not overweight, it's reasonable to offer her some ice cream or cake for dessert on occasion. But always buy or make just enough of the dessert to go around for that particular meal. Don't stock up as if for a famine or a flood when you might not be able to get to the store for a month. If you do, it will be too easy to give the baby more ice cream if she goes to bed on time.

One thing your baby definitely doesn't need *ever* is soda. Soda represents a lot of calories and no food value. It often replaces milk or juice which the baby needs and it starts her on the path to eating trash foods.

Apples vs. Lollipops

All of which brings me to the subject of snacks, another eating habit Americans have recently invented. My feeling is that nobody, including babies and children, needs to eat between meals. If a child eats three meals a day, that should be sufficient nourishment. She's usually not hungry for more. Of course, if she actually does get hungry (and it's not a figment of her mother's imagination), there's nothing wrong with a small snack. There *is* something wrong, however, with the wrong kind of snack. We have become a nation of trash eaters, consuming billions of tons of junk foods every year. And we're training our children from an early age to be the same.

If you really think your baby needs something to eat occasionally between meals, don't give her sweets. She doesn't need them, they'll make her fat, you'll pay for them in dental bills later on, you'll tamper with her appetite for her next meal. Give her a little genuine juice (not a fruit *drink*), a piece of raw fruit, a carrot stick, a stalk of celery, or a piece of whole-wheat bread. On occasion, perhaps a pretzel or a teething biscuit. If she's handed a banana or a piece of apple instead of a lollipop, she's going to take it, and she's going to be perfectly happy with it—if she hasn't become accustomed to the lollipop.

Just for fun one day, I checked the carriages and strollers of a few mothers who wheeled their babies to my office. It was amazing what provisions I found. These women were stocked up as if they were going on a camping trip to the Himalayas. There were large quantities of food—cookies, all varieties but mainly chocolate, pretzels, potato chips, candy. Not one piece of fruit, cheese or vegetable, though a few of them had taken some juice along on their expedition to the pediatrician.

Now, there's no reason to be frightened by a potato chip or horrified by chocolate cookies; I'm not saying a child should never taste these things. It won't hurt if, once in a while, she has a popsicle. But she shouldn't have them in the normal everyday course of events. This is the age when the habit of between-meal snacks usually gets firmly established. It's the time the cookie and the candy generally make the scene. It's the time when you should consciously resist the temptation to let your baby make a habit of it. And it's the time when the "tyranny of children" begins. Your little one knows how to let you know what she wants and she'll be the boss if you aren't strong enough to hold on to the responsibility of deciding what's eaten in your house.

Fatproof Your House

The best way to fatproof your child is to fatproof your house—get rid of all the non-nutritious junk foods that provide "empty calories" and little else. If these non-foods aren't at hand, you won't be tempted to feed them to your baby (or yourself). Later when the baby is old enough to forage for her own snacks, she'll find only the healthy kinds like fruit and cheese and juice. You won't have to insist, "Just two candies now, Tammy. You've already had enough," as she makes a grab for another handful or whines for more.

Though a baby of one to two years has some exposure to outside influences, 99 percent of the time *you* have absolute control over what she eats. It doesn't hurt if Grandma gives her cookies (if she doesn't live upstairs), or if the barber hands her a lollipop, because the usual baby doesn't escape from the house too often. There's no need to police the area so that no one ever offers her junk food. *But, at home during your normal activities, what the baby eats is your responsibility.* Remember that this is the time in your baby's life when her eating habits begin to be formed. If she's hooked on candy and cookies now, she'll probably always be hooked on them.

Train the Babysitters

Let me caution you about babysitters, housekeepers and live-in grandparents, however, because this group is noted, in my mind anyway, for their complete refusal to go along with the non-sweets decision. If you don't want your baby fed junk food, you must thoroughly impress this fact on anyone who takes care of the baby when you're not there.

Tell the person, "Here are some snacks you can give the baby if she needs something. Please don't give her *anything* else." And be sure your edict is followed.

I remember one baby who had both me and his parents baffled. At eighteen months of age, Jonathan had recently started gaining too much weight. We couldn't figure out why. Then one day his mother called me; she had the solution. She had started working three mornings a week and had hired a lovely grandmotherly sitter who evidently couldn't believe that Mrs. S. didn't feed the baby sweets. Not finding any around the house, she had taken to bringing her own supply. She wanted to be sure the baby would be happy to see her each morning.

It wasn't easy, but Mrs. S. managed to put a stop to the sweets and little Jonathan slimmed down again.

One of the most destructive ways of using junk foods, which your child doesn't need, is to offer them as "mood improvers," when she's unhappy, when she's making a fuss, crying, having a temper tantrum. "Stop crying, love. Here's a piece of nice candy." It usually works, but it teaches her to associate eating with feeling miserable and then feeling better.

Almost all obese people, it's been found, eat not when they're hungry but for external reasons, especially when they're depressed and upset. They get comfort from eating because they've been taught to associate the two. There are many other ways to comfort your baby besides food. That's the easy way out.

Our taste for sweets is conditioned, starting very early. A child who isn't given non-foods regularly doesn't end up having the same feeling about them later on. She won't crave them the way so many of us do. If she's offered sweets, she'll take some but she won't be tempted to munch her way through a whole chocolate cake or four candy bars. You won't have trained her to be a sugar freak.

The Bedtime Snack

Probably the worst time for a snack is at bedtime. That's another American tradition—the before-bed snack. In terms of the development of obesity, this is the most destructive habit we have. Whatever calories are taken in then are not burned up through activity and we wake up with them in the morning. Mothers seem to have the idea that their children need "a little something" to tide them over till breakfast. They don't. If your baby has eaten her supper at five or five-thirty, she won't be hungry at seven-thirty or eight when she goes to bed, because there hasn't been time for her stomach to empty. If you always give the baby that little something before she goes to bed, her cue for eating will be bedtime, not hunger.

With rare exceptions, the snack a child has before bed consists of sugar or starch, a high-calorie snack. Besides ruining her teeth, it gives her calories she doesn't need. As Dr. Richard F. Spark, assistant clinical professor of medicine at Harvard Medical School, wrote in the *New York Times* recently, a single Oreo cookie eaten every day for a year will put an extra two and a half pounds on an adult. It will put more on a baby.

He added, "If anything is to be done to decrease the prevalence of obesity in the next generation, the eating patterns of our children must be altered."

Meals with the Family

It's at about this age, between one and two, that many children begin eating with the family, at least for some meals. If it's possible to have the baby eat with you—if her father gets home early enough, if everyone is patient—I think it's a great idea. It's a time to be together, to have a feeling of closeness, and to teach your toddler good eating habits as well. That means, of course, that the meal is a pleasant experience for everybody, not a time to argue or criticize, or to wolf down the food placed before them. Many families tend to eat at breakneck speed, washing their food down with fluids, and this is certainly not a good influence on a baby who should learn to eat slowly, chew properly and take time to smell and taste the food.

The food should be placed on the table, everyone (including the baby) should eat as much as he or she wants, and that's all. No one is angry, no one is unhappy if the food isn't finished; no one is happy if it is. Often, as we all know, mealtime becomes a battleground, with the battle to see who wins—the mother if the baby finishes all her food, or the child if she's able to avoid eating the last spoonful. Eating shouldn't be a competition, nor should the child be urged to finish by, "See? Daddy finished his dinner!"

If a baby is to learn to eat healthily, then her family must eat that way too. If her brother chews on cookies all day and her father drinks coke for dinner, if her mother is addicted to ice-cream sandwiches, cooks and eats huge starchy meals, a baby will follow right along. So the best thing you can do is to change your own eating habits before she's old enough to do not as you *say,* but as you *do.*

Toddlers Need Exercise

Many parents have strange ideas about exercise and do everything they can to keep their babies from getting it. This not only reflects the parents' sedentary ways, but their concern that such young human beings are terribly fragile and need to be protected from physical strain. They worry that their baby will "overexert" herself, that she'll get "too tired," develop hernias, strain her heart, become bowlegged. They're obsessed with the possibility of an accident, so they cut off any opportunities for adventure. I constantly see children who have been prevented from getting outside for fear of hurting themselves.

This is complete nonsense. As I've stressed earlier when I discussed very young babies, exercise is healthy in every way and goes a long way toward keeping weight down. Your toddler should be encouraged to run rather than walk, and walk rather than ride or be carried. It's good for hearts to exercise; and hernias don't develop from good wholesome activity. The baby will sit down when she's tired. If she is permitted to get around on her own, she'll love it. She'd much rather do things than sit in one place—which usually turns out to be in front of the TV set with a big supply of cookies.

A child is naturally inquisitive and she likes to explore. She certainly doesn't have to explore the roof unattended, nor does she have to destroy the house, but, within limits, she should be allowed to move around and use her muscles. If she can walk, she should be given the opportunity to do a respectable amount of walking every day even though it's much easier to push her in a stroller. She'll be much healthier and happier, and the walking certainly won't hurt her mother either! If you realize that an hour of walking burns up 300 calories, you can see it will help keep the baby's weight down, as well as tone up her muscles. Sitting in front of the television set burns up no calories at all. Add the cookies she's eating there to the lack of activity and you've got a baby who's on the road to fat.

Children who don't get enough exercise are the ones who get flabby, sit more, eat more, become overweight and uncoordinated. As they become heavier, they become less active, and an unhealthy cycle has begun which in ten years will probably result in a fat, lethargic, unhappy adolescent.

The Overweight Baby

If, as you read this, your one- to two-year-old is already fat, too fat, according to her doctor and your eye, it means that until now she's taken in more calories than she's burned up. What you have to do now, in a modest way, is reduce the calories and increase the activity. You don't want to do anything drastic because she's growing and developing. You don't want her to lose weight, but merely to slow down her rate of weight *gain* till her height catches up with her weight.

Though your pediatrician is the only person who's qualified to tell you if your child is or isn't overweight, because body build must be taken into consideration, here are the *average* normal weights of two-year-olds of three different birth weights:

Birth weight:	6 pounds	$7\frac{1}{2}$ pounds	$8\frac{1}{2}$ pounds
Weight at two:	$23\frac{1}{4}$ pounds	27 pounds	31 pounds

No Diets for Toddlers

There's *no* reason to put a baby on a very strict diet. It's important not to interfere with her normal growth because if she doesn't get enough calories she will begin to burn up her own protein which can affect her development adversely. But you can keep her from gaining too rapidly.

Make a list of every bite she eats in a day. I think you'll be amazed at the number of unnecessary calories she's stowing away. The idea is to cut them down a little.

First of all, I would recommend, if your child has a large appetite and is gaining too fast, that you dilute her milk. I don't advocate skimmed milk yet unless she is tremendously overweight, though I do for older children. But you should dilute the whole milk with water so that she isn't taking in so many calories when she drinks.

Look at it this way: if your baby drinks, say, three eight-ounce glasses of milk a day, each containing 160 calories, she is consuming 480 calories a day in milk. If you dilute the milk, six ounces of milk to two ounces of water, you have reduced each glass by 40 calories or 120 a day, making a total intake of 360 calories. That's 3,600 *fewer* calories a month, equal to about a pound. So, if your baby has been gaining at a rate of one and a half pounds a month, she will now only gain half a pound, just by diluting her milk.

There's no way a child can gain too much on a diet mainly of meat, vegetables, and fruit. She can't consume enough to make her fat. Obviously, then, if your toddler is gaining too rapidly, I'd suggest cutting down on high-calorie foods, which include bread, spaghetti, potatoes, and cereals. You should give her some of these, but not excessive amounts.

But it's the between-meal eating that adds the pounds. If you keep in mind that four chocolate-chip cookies a day at 50 calories a cookie add up to 200 calories, then you'll realize that if you cut down to two cookies a day, you'll have taken off 100 calories. That's 3,000 calories a month, or a little under a pound of weight. Better still, cut the cookies out altogether.

You can see that it only requires small changes in the child's diet to affect real changes in weight gain. You'll be doing her a favor to do it now before her weight becomes a persistent problem for her.

In addition to cutting down food intake, encourage your overweight toddler to get more exercise so she'll tone up her muscles and burn calories at the same time. Don't push her or carry her—let her walk and run. Use the playpen only when you must. If she watches television (and I admit TV is too great a temptation for most mothers to resist—it is a handy way for them to get some rest when they have a toddler who's into everything), don't plop her down with a fistful of cookies. She'll be happy with a carrot or a banana to chew on. She may even be happy with a toy instead of food.

The fat child, even at one or one and a half, is already less active than a thin child. She doesn't walk as fast or as far. She's much more likely to sit more. As you begin to slow down her rate of weight gain, you'll see that she'll feel like doing more in a more coordinated way. She'll have more fun. And, in turn, her increased activity will help keep her weight down.

The only ones who can establish or change your child's eating and exercise patterns are you, her parents. The time is now, while your baby is young, while she eats only what you give her, before her fat cells have irrevocably increased, to start her on the road to being thin and help her acquire a taste for healthy foods.

If you can prevent your baby from being fat at two, she'll have a much better chance of not having to battle the bulge later in her life—the bulge that brings with it so many physical ills and emotional problems. You'll have shown your love, not by feeding her too much, but by keeping her thin.

Check your child's risk of being fat forever on the appropriate chart on page 65. You will see that if she's got two overweight parents and is fat herself at two, she has a high risk of becoming a fat adult. Without the fat parents, she has only a moderate risk if she's always been over-weight. Your job is to reduce even that moderate risk as much as you can.

10

The Preschool Child: Almost the Last Chance to Slim Down

Scoring the Risk at 2 Years

One fat parent .... 2 points
Two fat parents .... 4 points
Fat at 1 year .... 2 points
Fat at 2 years .... 2 points

Your child's total .... ―――――

0–2 points means your child has a low risk of
future fat.
4 points means he has a moderate risk.
6–8 points means he has a high risk.

Scoring the Risk at 6 Years

One fat parent .... 2 points
Two fat parents .... 4 points
Fat at 1 year .... 2 points
Fat at 2 years .... 2 points
Fat at 6 years .... 2 points

Your child's total .... ―――――

0–2 points means your child has a low risk of
ending up fat.
4–6 points means he has a moderate risk.
8–10 points means he has a high risk.

By the time your child is about two, much has been decided
in your house. Among other things, the way he eats now is
the way he's probably always going to eat unless you make a
real effort to change it. And whether he's fat or thin now
may well be the way he's always going to be, as an
adolescent and as an adult, unless you make a strenuous
effort to change that. As I've stressed, eating patterns are
established very early in a child's life, and so is his
disposition for slimness or obesity.

If you've stuffed your baby with food, allowed him to
become overweight and preoccupied with eating, and have
led him to confuse food with love, all is not lost, however.
Though it does become more difficult to alter the trend as a
child gets older, there is still plenty of time for you to do it
now, and manage to send a nice slender child off to first
grade at five or six. But, I would venture to say that if you
do not want your child to grow up battling fat, *now is
almost your last chance* to make your stand. If he's still
overweight at five or six, then your problems will evermore
be much more difficult to handle.

In the years between two and six, from the age of two,
when your child is no longer a baby, till he goes to school,
food likes and dislikes are firmly established, eating habits
become almost irrevocably set, and you and your pediatrician must decide if it's necessary to change them. In a
youngster who does not take in more calories than he burns
up, it's been shown that the production of new fat cells will
increase at a normal rate until he is about two. Then there
will be little increase in these cells till around the age of ten
when production picks up again. In a child who eats too
much and gains too rapidly, they will continue to increase
after two, resulting in larger-than-normal numbers of fat
cells which will always be more than eager to stuff
themselves full. So these are important years.

Dr. Jerome Knittle, the fat-cell expert, has found that by

age six a certain number of obese children already have a greater number of fat cells than many normal adults. These fat cells, he asserts, will remain with them forever, making them susceptible to overweight for the rest of their lives.

Other nutritionists pose the theory that eating too much encourages excess fat storage in children who are genetically susceptible to it. Others stress that years of overeating produce an almost irreversible habit of overeating.

Whatever the reason, if your child is decidedly fat at five, and especially if fat seems to run in the family, if you and/or your spouse are overweight, there's an excellent chance— one estimate is four out of five—that the child will be fat as an adolescent and as an adult. If, however, he's been overweight earlier than five or six and slims down by that age, he is much more likely to remain slim later in his life. Check the appropriate scoring box at the beginning of this chapter to find out his current chances of turning into a perennially overweight adult.

In one study of 100 obese adolescents, it was found that forty-five of them had been fat by the time they were six. In another study, 85 percent of fat adults admitted to being far overweight at five.

It's Not Healthy to Be Fat

We know today that the old wives' tales were wrong. It is not true that plumpness is a measure of good health. We know now that a *thin* child is the healthiest child, and that a thin child has the best chance of always maintaining a normal weight. Many people still feel that a chubby little three-year-old is the cutest, the cuddliest, as well as the healthiest because "he has reserves against illness." But I have found that markedly overweight children have a higher incidence of illness, especially respiratory infections. And being fat isn't so cute when you realize it can be lethal later on in life. An obese adult is much more likely than a slender one to develop high blood pressure, arteriosclerosis, heart attacks, diabetes, and other serious diseases. And, by the time a chubby toddler turns into a fat child of five or six, he's not so cute any more.

Somehow, many parents want to have fat babies and toddlers, but then they want slim school-agers and adolescents. This makes no sense at all. You can't have it both ways. Those fat babies, if they don't slim down before they enter school, are probably going to be *fat* school-agers and adolescents. They're in the habit of eating more than their bodies require, and their fat cells have probably irrevocably overmultiplied.

So, my advice is to decide *early* to send an attractively slender child off to his first day at school. Hopefully, he's been thin since birth but, if he hasn't, you must slim him down now in the preschool years. Unfortunately, I don't see this happening often enough. This upsets me terribly and it should upset you as well.

"Doctor, He Eats Like a Bird."

If you're willing to make the effort, nature will help you. Normally the appetite of a child at around two, and continuing for a number of years after, drops off even more than it did before. At two and after, a child tends to want to eat less because he is not growing as fast now and doesn't need as much food. Physiologically, this is a time when fewer calories are required.

Psychologically, however, it's a time when many parents, fearing illness, "lowered resistance," even malnutrition, start with the coaxing and the carrying on over eating. They are panicked by the normal physiologic decrease in appetite.

The fact is, more children in America today suffer from *super*nutrition than malnutrition. They are overfed, over-nourished, and *fat*.

I suggest taking advantage of your child's normal decrease in appetite. Feed him only as much as he wants. Though you may tie mother love in with feeding your child, you'll be doing him a much greater service to let his untampered-with appetite take charge. If he's healthy and thin, he'll continue to be. If he's become too heavy, he'll start to slim down while continuing to grow as he should.

Everything I've said in earlier chapters about feeding your baby holds true for preschoolers too. Don't insist that your preschooler overeat. Put the food down on the table in front of him, let him eat as much of it as he wants, then take the plate away without judgment. No "What a good boy, he's eaten all his dinner," or "You're making me very sad because you're not finishing your carrots." Relax and stop worrying. However much he's eaten for that meal, Mommy isn't upset.

Your Child Won't Starve

That's not easy. I know it isn't. I know from the mothers who come to me and from my own experience with my own children. One of my mothers called me just this morning to say, "I've tried to take your advice and not get upset when Sharon doesn't eat. But I do get very upset, and I'm sure I show it even when I try not to. Last night, for example, she ate a couple of bites of meat, about four string beans, and that's all, except for some milk. After all, Dr. Eden, that's just not enough."

"Sure, that's enough. It's plenty," I answered. "She wasn't very hungry. When she is, she'll eat more. Her weight is just about right for her height and she's growing normally. Sharon's not starving. Don't push her to eat more than she wants."

I explained to Mrs. S. that Sharon, who is just over two, is perfectly normal. Her appetite has decreased just as it's supposed to at her age, and the best thing her mother can do is to stop worrying about it. My advice was to offer Sharon a well-balanced nutritious diet, tastefully prepared, and then relax. I warned against giving Sharon sweets and cookies and soda to "get a little nourishment into her," because it won't. It will give her only calories. And it will decrease her desire for nutritious food. Sharon will eat as much as she needs. When she's hungry, she'll eat more; when she's not, she'll eat less. And she won't waste away by morning.

I spend a lot of time every day trying to convince the mothers (and sometimes fathers) of my youthful patients that their preschoolers, who to them don't seem to be getting enough to eat, are not going to suffer. I tell them that a child's appetite should be the key to the amount of food he eats and not his parent's loving but misguided wishes to stuff him with good nourishing food. Once I've determined by a thorough examination that the child is in good physical shape and is growing normally, I explain how important it is for a young child not to get fat, tell them the stakes are high.

"I Worked So Hard. Eat It!"

Even for a mother who understands perfectly (intellectually) that her toddler will eat enough if it's presented to him, it's hard for her to be casual about it. It's hard to refrain from coaxing and enticing the child to eat that delicious dinner which took so much time to prepare and which he is now picking around at. Most mothers I know have felt like saying, and sometimes have actually said, "How can you do this to me? I worked so hard making your dinner, and now you won't eat it." That's perfectly understandable, because it *is* frustrating.

All I can tell you is that your child will end up in better shape, both in weight and in his relationship with you, if you can manage to put the food on the table and take it away when he loses interest in it, however much has been eaten, with no fuss at all. If you can be relaxed about it, whether he eats everything or only a bite or two, you'll have gone a long way towards keeping him thin and healthy. You won't have made him associate food with your love, or your anger, or your anxiety, and overstuff himself to make you happy. You won't have made him connect eating with being a "good boy." Children are very anxious to please their parents (though it may not always seem that way), and even if it means stuffing themselves to the ears when they don't want to, they'll try to do it for *you*.

Fussy Eaters

Many, in fact, most, children at this age are very fussy about their food, and most of their mothers worry about it. But as long as a child gets some of the four basic foods every day, along with a multivitamin, it doesn't matter whether he will eat only hamburgers and chicken, milk, carrots and peas, cereal and sliced pears every single day of the week. Gradually he will pick up more foods he likes, especially if you don't make a fuss and if you don't fill him up instead on empty calories.

Vegetables, in particular, tend to be a hangup for both child and mother. Mrs. H. called up frantically one morning during my advice hour, terribly worried about her three-year-old. For the past three days, he hadn't eaten a green vegetable. What should she do? I explained that if he didn't eat a green vegetable for three months it wouldn't matter since she gave him daily vitamins. I encouraged her to serve vegetables every day but not to fight with him about eating them. Eventually he would begin on his own.

Don't Start Nagging

It's easy now, if you're not watchful, to begin a tug of war between you and your small child which could color your entire relationship and exist for the rest of your lives. It's important not to set up a situation where the child refuses to do something—in this case, eat—and you respond by nagging.

"I don't want it."

"Come on, down the hatch!"

"I'm full."

"Just a little more, that's a good boy."

"No!"

"You're upsetting Mommy. Eat your dinner all up now."

A child soon learns to tune out a nagging parent, or to go along for the sake of peace, or to be defiant. And the stress begins to mount. If you'll take my advice, you won't let the nagging syndrome get a foothold in your relationship. It doesn't work, it's unpleasant for everyone, and it may contribute to the making of a fat child.

Families Who Eat Together

Many parents ask me when a child should start eating with the rest of the family. I think the sooner the better, as long as everyone enjoys it. There's no harm in a preschooler eating dinner at 6:00 or 7:00—if he doesn't become overly tired and cranky—if that's when the rest of the family sits down. One mother who'd religiously, since the time her child was born, fed him at 5:00 and had him in pajamas by 6:00, was aghast when I told her that. "That's too late for him," she said.

But I don't think it's unreasonable to feed a four-year-old at 7:00, if his father gets home that late. If he's in bed by 8:00 or 8:30, he'll get as much sleep as he needs. Besides, eating dinner at that hour will cut out the "need" for cookies and milk at bedtime which give him calories he won't burn up while he sleeps.

I'm not saying that this works out for all families—you have to make your own decisions. Recently I suggested to the mother of a five-year-old that he eat with the family at 6:30 when the father came home. I made a mistake in this case because this particular mother is a compulsive sort of person and if I said 6:30, that was the law, that was dinnertime for Jimmy.

Three months later, when she brought Jimmy to my office for an examination, I asked her how the new dinner hour was working out. It wasn't working out at all. Jimmy was overtired by 6:30, she said, and managed to disrupt everybody's meal.

OK, I said, then feed him earlier. Many five-year-olds can manage to wait, and many can't. But I do feel that meals should be family affairs just as soon as it works out nicely.

Mealtime—at this age and any age—should be a pleasant time, with no rush, no arguing, no pressure, no competitions with Daddy to see who cleans his plate first. Meals are a time to be together and to talk with one another in a relaxed atmosphere. They should be slow and leisurely with time for conversation and discussions of the day's activities—your little child's included. Remember what I've said earlier: If the family eats at an excessively rapid clip, one course right after another, the food wolfed down, children will learn to eat that way too, a big step on the road to obesity.

One supereffective way to turn what should be pleasant

get-togethers into tension and hassling is to keep at your child about eating all the food on his plate. It's also a supereffective way to train him to overeat.

Keep Portions Small

I suggest giving a small child small portions. Most people overestimate the amount of food a young child needs, pile enormous portions on his plate, and then push him to eat it. If you give smaller portions, you can always give seconds if he wants them. This will take the pressure off both the child and you and make everyone at the table happier. Give him a little of everything, the vegetables included, and then sit down and enjoy your own dinner. If a child has learned by age two or three that the eating experience is pleasant, that he can eat as much or as little as he wants, he'll seldom have a weight problem later on. And he'll have far fewer emotional problems as well.

Mealtime Is for Eating

Most of the food eaten in your house ideally should be eaten *at mealtime*, together as a family group and sitting down at the table. Many families today find it less and less possible to eat this way because of busy schedules and differing time tables. And many people, children included, tend to eat hurry-up, catch-as-catch-can breakfasts and lunches containing little real nourishment, then nibble all day long until they arrive at dinner time when, *perhaps*, a real meal appears, only to be followed by more nibbling.

When I was talking recently with the mother and father of Janet, one of my five-year-old patients, I learned that a meal together in their house was an event, usually occurring on Sunday. At other times, everyone fixed his own breakfast, grabbed lunch from the refrigerator at home, or ate at school, or ate out. Everyone even had his dinner separately because Daddy came home from work very late, the two teen-agers usually wanted to rush off to basketball practice or play rehearsals, leaving Mommy and Janet on their own. The little girl, who was decidedly overweight, was obviously stuffing herself on foods of her choice which consisted, it seemed to me, mostly of canned ravioli and bread.

I did my best to impress upon the parents that Janet needed the right foods at the right times (so did everyone else, for that matter), and set up a schedule for meals with a menu plan. The last time I spoke to Janet's mother, the arrangement seemed to be working out excellently.

I suggest making every attempt to make the three real meals as much of an everyday ritual as you can manage, given your particular situation, with three defined times to sit down together to eat (even if just you and your one small child happen to be the only members of the family available at the time).

A Well-Balanced Diet

While a child should be allowed to decide how *much* to eat at meals, you must decide the *kinds* of food you serve. The three meals a day must, if your aim is to bring up a thin, healthy child, include—again without absolute rigidity—the following foods:

Two servings of meat, fish or eggs (no more than 3 or 4 eggs a week). Alternates might be cooked dry beans, peas or lentils, peanut butter, cottage cheese, hard cheeses.

Four or more servings of vegetables and fruits, including

at least one dark green vegetable, one yellow vegetable and one citrus fruit.

Two or three 8-ounce glasses of milk. Alternates: cottage cheese, cheddar-type cheese, ice cream, yogurt. The milk may be whole, skimmed, buttermilk, evaporated, reconstituted dry milk.

Four servings of breads and cereals. These include whole-grain or enriched bread, cereals (non-sugar-coated), pasta, rice, oats, cornmeal.

One multivitamin pill, though the child who eats a truly well-balanced diet doesn't require it.

I've explained the value of all these body-building foods in Chapter 6. Each has its importance in a child's diet, and you should offer them every day—without any pressure to eat them all up.

I do suggest, though, that you do your best to feed the child fruits and vegetables at times when he's hungriest. These are the foods that most Americans, who eat notoriously poor diets today, tend to shun. If you can foster a liking for them in your child at an early age, he'll always like them.

Begin now serving a "prudent" low-cholesterol diet, with emphasis on poultry, fish and veal instead of red meat and too many eggs. A child of about six should begin to drink skimmed milk instead of whole, whether or not he is thin or already overweight. Cut out the saturated fats (which include animal fats and hardened vegetable fats) as much as possible, substituting the polyunsaturated varieties (liquid vegetable oils such as corn, safflower and soybean oils). Read the labels! This diet won't harm your child and it may save him from high blood pressure or a heart attack many years from today.

At the same time, remember, now as when your toddler was an infant, refrain from sprinkling too much sugar or too much salt on his food. Remember that excessive sugar will make him fat, replace the foods he needs, and lead to problems later in life, while excessive salt can encourage high blood pressure. Now is the time to train your child to eat for a healthy future.

Switch the Snacks

Now let me get to the subject of snacks, which is where most of us go astray, allowing our children to decide what they're going to eat and when they're going to eat it.

Constant snacking is a habit we all have fallen into in recent years. Somehow we feel we can't make it through the day on only three meals. Coffee breaks are an institution for adults, and "a little something" to tide them over till lunch or dinner or the next morning is an institution for our children.

Since I certainly don't think I can convince many parents that small children (or large ones either) don't need to nibble all day long, I am going to try to convince them to substitute healthy snacks for junk or sweets. If your preschool child asks for something to eat between meals, give him a piece of fruit, a carrot stick, a slice of hard cheese. Perhaps some juice or skimmed milk. Or how about a glass of water? Many parents never think of giving children water when they're thirsty. Note: They *never* need soda.

Often the child won't be hungry at all, merely irritable or fussy for some reason other than hunger. I would venture to say that this is true most of the time, because your child's stomach cannot be empty—and therefore require food—for at least three hours after he's eaten a meal. Perhaps some cuddling, some new activity, some attention, some time to himself, is what he needs, not food. If you always improve his mood with food, he'll learn to eat whenever he's bored, unhappy, or discontent. I'm sure you know many fat adults who do the same. They learned how when they were children.

A big temptation many—probably most—parents have is to bribe their children to eat or reward them for doing so with junk foods. "Eat your dinner and I'll give you a nice piece of candy." That's wrong for a lot of reasons.

First, it tempts them to eat more than they want to, giving them one kind of food in return for eating other kinds of food.

Second, it teaches them to associate sweet foods, often completely non-nutritive, with approval.

Third, it trains them to covet food that can make them fat and miserable. It can produce children—and I've seen many—who eat a lot but are undernourished.

And last, feeding your child non-food defeats your purpose of getting him to take in enough nourishment—it will fill him up, make him fat perhaps, but it won't contribute to his small body's needs.

Dr. Neal Solomon, the well-known nutritionist on the staff of Johns Hopkins University Medical School, says, "Study indicates the desire to eat sweets often stems from an early age when the parent typically offered candy to comfort or bribe a child."

Good Boys Get Lollipops

Sweets as positive reinforcers for good behavior are to be avoided at all costs. Unless you consciously restrain yourself from offering your small child a lollipop or a chocolate cookie to ward off a temper tantrum or to keep him quiet, or to eat his dinner, or to calm him down, you are bribing him to behave. He'll quickly learn that the way to get treats is to make a fuss. I have to admit I am guilty of a certain amount of bribery myself. To keep the noise down to a roar in my office, I give out lollipops—granted they're sugarless lollipops, but lollipops all the same. I do it for the same reasons mothers do it—to keep the little ones quiet and to reward them for "good" behavior. As I write this, I realize I'll have to mend my ways.

There's nothing wrong with candy, ice cream, cookies or any of the other sweet foods—once in a while. There *is* something wrong with them as a daily routine.

My experience is that when children are exposed to nourishing, body-building foods like vegetables, salads, cheeses, meats, fruits, cereals—without unfair competition from Ring Dings, marshmallow cupcakes and lollipops—these will become the foods they like. These will be the foods they want. Certainly, they'll also like ice cream, cake, cookies, and candy. There's no reason not to give them these things occasionally. Ice cream or chocolate pudding for dessert now and then, a piece of candy on a special occasion, a Ring Ding or a cupcake with chocolate icing and sprinkles from time to time won't harm your child or make him fat. But as a steady diet they probably will, and, in any case, they won't do him any good.

They'll probably ruin his teeth too. Doctors working in the Northwest Territories among the Eskimos have found that these people who a few years ago had universally healthy teeth are now having horrendous dental problems. This is attributed to their change in diet since the white man has invaded their lands and influenced their eating habits away from a diet largely limited to whale, caribou and seal meats to one that includes candy, cookies, and soda pop.

Preschoolers Are Homebodies

Most preschoolers spend just about all of their time at home, or not too far from it, perhaps with time out for nursery school. So most of the food they eat is eaten right there, under your supervision, before your very eyes. This makes it easy for you to give your child the kind of food he needs.

I do, however, recall a consultation with one of my mothers who had a markedly overweight four-year-old. I told her the responsibility for what he ate and didn't eat rested with her because this little fellow wasn't eating in school yet and he wasn't big enough to patronize the candy store or ice-cream parlor by himself. Wrong. Billy's mother had a job and the boy spent his day at his grandmother's house. My next step was to speak to Grandma, but I didn't get very far with her. From the old school and fat herself, Grandma was absolutely certain—and there seemed no way to change her resolute mind—that Billy was perfect just the way he was. I left the problem in his mother's hands, suggesting that all-day nursery school might be the solution. But when I last saw Billy for a checkup, his configurations had changed very little. I seriously doubt that he'll ever be thin.

Who's in charge in your house? Who decides what little Jimmy is going to eat, you or Jimmy? It had better be you, because your preschooler will learn in a hurry, if he hasn't already, if you've given the job to him.

Children at two, three, four, and five are increasingly verbal, and can tell you just what they want and don't want. They have definite likes and dislikes. If you let them decide, they'll eat potato chips instead of salad, soda pop in place of milk. If you let them choose to nibble all day long on candy and corn chips interspersed with chocolate cookies, you and they are on the road to disaster. If they're making these important decisions now, think what your lives will be like when they are adolescents. And fat, at that.

"Mommy, Buy Me Some!"

Although children in the preschool years do most of their eating at home, they are already affected by outside influences. Probably the biggest of these is television which presents children's programs in between commercials for junk food. I've never seen a commercial for broiled fish or apples or carrot sticks or baked chicken, but I've certainly seen them for sugar-coated cereals, chocolate candies that won't stick to your hands, potato chips and marshmallow-filled cupcakes made mostly out of chemicals. Small children, unfortunately, spend tremendous numbers of hours (one estimate is five hours a day) in front of the TV being brainwashed by advertisers to tell their mommies to buy cock-a-doodle-doos or sugar-coated yumyums the next time they go to the supermarket. Of course they'll want them. And of course they'll put the pressure on to buy them.

Outside Influences on Your Child's Eating Habits

Children find out very early that a visit to the barber shop or the shoe store (or the doctor's office!) will produce lollipops. Grandma, along with Uncle Ben and Aunt Susan, will always have a supply of brownies and soda and gumdrops. So will their young friends' mothers. I remember my daughter coming home one day from the next-door neighbor's house proclaiming that "They always have such good things to eat at Fran's house. Her mommy is real nice. She doesn't give us apples to eat."

One patient's mother told me that her little girl said to her, "It's much more fun to go to Chris's house. She always has candy for us. Why don't we ever have good things here?"

Her child's friend, by the way, is a patient of mine, and is certainly one of the fattest children in my practice.

The Child as Tyrant

Not long ago, Mrs. L. came to my office to tell me that she was at the end of her rope. Her four-year-old son was a little dictator who had quite literally taken over their house. All was chaos unless Jason got what he wanted. The child at four was many, many pounds overweight. That was because, I discovered, the only way his parents could avoid complete destruction of their house and sanity was to keep on hand a never-ending supply of the exact foods, announced by brand name, the boy demanded (learned from TV, no doubt).

As this was a new patient and I didn't know Jason's past history, I asked his mother to tell me. Jason had been born prematurely to parents who had been awaiting a child for eleven years. He weighed only three and a half pounds at birth. Mrs. L., terribly worried about him, was desperate that he get enough food and gain weight quickly. As a result, she spent her life doing literally anything to make him eat. He gained weight, much too much, and he gained complete control of the household as well.

Jason and his mother are, of course, an extreme case of what's been called "juvenarchy," the reign of children. But to a lesser degree, most of us are guilty of the same sort of parental collapse, especially where food is concerned.

Handling the Pressure

A four- or five-year-old can put on a lot of pressure, and it takes strength and belief in what you're doing to resist it. But resist you must, quietly, without making a big deal of it, especially if your child is already gaining weight too rapidly. Once he knows the rules, and you're consistent about them, he'll accept them.

I'm often asked how to handle the pressure from little children. I think it's best merely to say, "Those things aren't good to eat and we don't eat them here." The explanations will soon become unnecessary—and your child *won't* stop loving you because you don't go along with everyone else.

To make life easier, I suggest you fatproof your house, getting rid of all the calorie-ridden low-nutrition junk foods. If you have them lying around the house, filling your cupboards, you're sure to offer them too often. Your child will know they're there and he'll want them, that is certain. Be consistent—don't clear them out one day and buy them the next. Get out of the habit of handing out junk foods.

I'm not advocating running a militant household where sugar nibbles and candy never darken your door. Stopping off occasionally for an ice-cream cone or serving chocolate cake for dessert once in a while, buying cookies at the bakery now and then, isn't going to turn your child into a sugar freak. But binges of cones and candy sticks and cupcakes every day definitely will. And so will junk foods stocked in for a famine. They will also make your child fat.

And I'm not advocating taking a rigid position on junk food eaten outside the house. There's no sense warning all the mothers in your neighborhood not to feed your child. There's no point trying to make sure your child refuses lollipops from the shoe-store clerk or cookies from Grandma. Just be sure the food in *your* house is healthy.

Burning Up the Calories

One of the best ways to keep your child at a normal weight, as I've emphasized, is to be sure he gets enough exercise. Inactive children have no way to burn up the calories they take in and they're almost sure to become overweight. Once they're appreciably overweight, they'll exercise less because it will be harder to move around.

At this age, between two and six, children not only develop eating patterns but they develop exercise patterns as well. A child who's sedentary now may well always avoid any activity that requires an output of energy. Encourage yours to be as active as possible. Buy him a tricycle, give him enough leeway outdoors to run, go to the local pool in a family group to swim together, play ball, have races, go ice skating. And avoid regularly plunking him down for hours in front of the television set where the only exercise he'll get is an occasional trip to the bathroom or the refrigerator.

Preschool children are normally adventurous and love to run around, play games, explore the world. If you are overly protective, careful not to let your toddler get too tired, keeping him always safely at your side, worrying he'll get dirty or fall down and get hurt, he's not going to have the chance to develop coordination and other skills. What's more, he's probably going to get fat. Within reasonable limits, let your toddler run and climb and jump and play. When he gets tired, he'll stop.

If only for the exercise, giving him chores around the house is a good idea. Helping to make beds, running errands, sweeping, and raking will all use up calories that would otherwise turn to fat. So will walking instead of riding. Pushing a small child in a stroller does give more peace of mind—he's parked right there in front of you where you can always find him. And you can cover more ground more quickly. But he needs to use his own muscles, and walking is a good way to do it.

I remember a mother who arrived in my office on a hot day huffing and puffing and looking ready to collapse. She'd carried her three-year-old who weighed forty-five pounds from her car a couple of blocks away. I asked her why she hadn't let him walk. "He's so little," she said. "It would be too much for him in this heat." Nonsense, of course, but she couldn't see it that way.

Leave the car at home as much as you can, and walk wherever you're going. Or at least park the car a couple of blocks away, and walk from there. You might enjoy it, and *both* of you will be getting exercise.

The Already-Fat Preschooler

If your preschooler, for whatever reasons, has managed to become too heavy, now is the perfect time to start remedying the situation. Though it will be more difficult now than it would have been when he was a baby, that doesn't mean the battle is lost. And it will be easier to win at this point than if you wait any longer. It does mean a lot of things have to change. Right now.

What must change? The *way* your child eats and *what* he eats, along with the amount of exercise he gets. Your attitude. The attitude of the rest of the family. A little child who is too fat cannot be made responsible for slimming himself down. He isn't motivated to do it because he doesn't realize what his problem is; and even if he did, he is not mature enough to change. You, the parents, must make the change for him, and the whole family must cooperate if it's going to work.

It is not necessary, nor is it desirable, for a little child to lose a lot of weight in a hurry. In fact, it's usually not necessary for him to lose weight at all, but merely to slow down his rate of gain while his growth catches up with his weight. Occasionally, of course, a tremendously obese child will actually have to lose pounds. But always very, very slowly so that normal growth is not affected.

The first step to take, of course, is fatproofing your house as I've just described. It will take you fifteen minutes to get rid of all the unnecessary foods stashed in your pantry and kitchen cabinets. Don't hide them away and dole them out less frequently than you did before—get rid of them altogether, every crumb. Remember, if your child is fat, something has gone wrong. He's been eating too much of the wrong foods. If the cookies are still in the cabinet, you're asking too much of yourself and the child to resist. Eliminate the stocks of lollipops used for emergency purposes, give away the boxes of chocolate-covered ice-cream pops, dump the cookies. Skimmed milk should now completely replace whole milk.

Between meals, if your child is hungry, give him non-fattening snacks, like carrots and cheese, fruit, or skimmed milk. He'll soon get used to them—*if* you believe in what you're doing and you do it wholeheartedly. He won't suffer, and soon you won't either. You're not depriving him of love. You're depriving him of *fat.*

Everybody's in It Together

Mothers often ask me what to do about a fat child when there are other *thin* children in the house. My answer is to do just what I've described. A thin child shouldn't eat the junk foods either—they won't do him any good and they'll take away his appetite for the food he should eat. I recommend skimmed milk for almost everyone, but if you're uncertain, check with your own pediatrician.

I was discussing this recently with a family who had a very fat five-year-old boy, a rather thin thirteen-year-old older brother, and two normal parents. The mother was very anxious to have the younger one slim down. When I told her that she must, first of all, fatproof the house, she said, "But Doctor Eden, what about the rest of the family? Do we all have to suffer? Why can't I just watch what Jimmy eats?"

"Because it won't work," I told her. "You're all going to have to be in this together. What you'll be doing is establishing the proper nutritional environment for your child. If the rest of you keep on eating the way you have been, Jimmy will do it too. You can't expect him to follow a diet, avoiding some foods that are right there in the kitchen. He'll be frustrated and upset seeing everyone else having what he can't have. He'll feel punished for something that isn't his fault. It's not fair and it won't work, because you'll be sorry for him and you'll start backsliding more and more.

"My advice is, if you can't all agree to work this out, then it's better not to try it right now."

I firmly believe that, because that's the way it has worked out in my experience. I've had a high success rate among my patients, almost without exception, when everyone in the family has cooperated. When a child is treated separately, when everything he eats involves a big decision, then it usually does not work out.

No "Diets" Needed

Aside from cutting down on the between-meal nibbling, except for healthy snacks, you can cut down a certain number of calories—if it seems necessary—in your child's three meals. I am not talking about a crash diet; these are never good, especially for children. And I am not discussing medication, which has no place at all in a normal child's life. Merely a slowdown in calorie intake.

• Substitute skimmed milk (not "skimmed milk products" which contain less fat but almost as many calories as whole milk) for whole milk. An eight-ounce glass of skimmed milk contains 80 to 90 calories, "milk products" such as Light 'n Lively about 116 calories, and whole milk 160 calories.

• Don't make whole meals out of starch foods, like spaghetti, macaroni and cheese, ravioli, or potato pancakes.

• Substitute protein for pancakes, fruit for cake or pudding.

• Hold back on the butter and syrup, and sprinkle only a little sugar on cereals that need it.

• Even with your overweight child, there's no need to be rigid about sweets outside the house. An occasional ice-cream cone or cookie won't hurt. But most fat children, I've found, are accustomed to constant consumption of "treats." And so, usually, are their mothers. Don't make a stop at the candy store part of your daily routine.

• Along with a slowdown in the amount of fattening food eaten, get your child up and moving. Encourage him to get exercise in whatever way you can, as I described earlier in this chapter. As overweight children lose weight, they are more interested in exercise, and more able.

On the following page are given the average normal weights of children at ages two, three, four, five and six, depending on their birth weights (generally, the heavier at birth, the heavier a child will always be).

Check your preschooler's weight with the figures below to see whether he is too fat now. Then figure out his risk score from the appropriate box on page 65, to get a rough indication of whether or not he is shaping up to be fat all his life long. If he looks like he has a high risk of becoming a fat adult, it's advisable to get to work right now so that by the

AVERAGE NORMAL WEIGHTS

Birth Weight:	6 lbs	7½ lbs	8½ lbs
Two years:	23½ lbs	27 lbs	31 lbs
Three years:	27½ lbs	32 lbs	37 lbs
Four years:	31 lbs	36 lbs	43 lbs
Five years:	35 lbs	40 lbs	49 lbs
Six years:	39 lbs	46 lbs	54 lbs

time your youngster goes off to school he'll have slimmed down and edged into the moderate- or even low-risk category.

The earlier the better, but *any*time is a good time to begin.

11

School-Age Children: A Time for Real Concern

Scoring the Risk at 6 Years

One fat parent . . . . 2 points
Two fat parents . . . . 4 points
Fat at 1 year . . . . 2 points
Fat at 2 years . . . . 2 points
Fat at 6 years . . . . 2 points

Your child's total . . . . ————

0–2 points means your child has a low risk of ending up fat.
4–6 points means she has a moderate risk.
8–10 points means she has a high risk.

Scoring the Risk at 10 Years

One fat parent . . . . 2 points
Two fat parents . . . . 4 points
Fat at 1 year . . . . 2 points
Fat at 2 years . . . . 2 points
Fat at 6 years . . . . 2 points
Fat at 10 years . . . . 2 points

Your child's total . . . . ————

0–4 points puts her at low risk of becoming a fat adult.
6–8 points makes her a moderate risk.
10–12 points makes her a high risk.

Scoring the Risk at 12 Years

One fat parent . . . . 2 points
Two fat parents . . . . 4 points
Fat at 1 year . . . . 2 points
Fat at 2 years . . . . 2 points
Fat at 6 years . . . . 2 points
Fat at 10 years . . . . 2 points
Fat at 12 years . . . . 2 points

Your child's total . . . . _____

0–4 points makes her a low risk for becoming a fat adult.
6–10 points makes her a moderate risk.
12–14 points makes her a high risk.

It's not until a child starts going to school that many parents begin, for the first time, to be seriously concerned about her weight. When the rolypoly baby, the adorable chubby toddler, doesn't miraculously turn into an acceptably slender child, they come to the realization that maybe something is wrong. Chances are if a child has been and still is fat by the age of six or so, she'll be that way the rest of her life if her parents continue to wait for miracles. (Check the most appropriate scoring box above to find out your school child's potential for forever having a weight problem.)

While it's certainly possible, and definitely an excellent idea, to slim down an overweight six- or seven-year-old, I can tell you as a pediatrician that it's a much tougher job than it would have been earlier in your child's life. A child who has grown up thin from infancy *with good eating habits and plenty of exercise* will probably never be fat. And if both parents have always been thin, so much the better. Though she may have an occasional bout with a few extra pounds, it's not very likely this child will tend always to be overweight.

But if she's been consuming too much of the wrong foods all of her short life, would much prefer sitting around to riding her bike, and especially if she was born to overweight parents, then both of you are undoubtedly in for more of a struggle. A child of six or eight who has always been overweight may have developed, according to some nutritionists, a supersupply of fat cells that will never again disappear and will always make it hard for her to keep her weight under control. Her eating habits are probably quite firmly established, her likes and dislikes distinct. Her distaste for physical activity is pronounced. The truth is, it gets harder to fight fat every year as she grows older.

There's Time for a Change

But there is still time for her to grow up thin, *if* you start making changes *now*. You can stop the multiplication of fat cells which in a normally slim child do not increase in number from about the age of two till around ten, but which continue to increase in an overweight child. You can stop the fat-cell multiplication right now by making certain that your youngster does not keep on gaining weight at such a rapid rate. It won't be easy because, obviously, you and she have developed bad habits.

Fat Isn't Fun

I have never met a fat person, child or adult, who enjoys being fat, though I've met a few who've settled for it. I've never met a fat person who likes what she sees when she looks in the mirror. I've never met a fat person who really thinks well of herself. I've talked to many obese children, of all ages, who are miserable because they are not acceptable to their peers or their elders, are unable to participate in normal activities, and are discriminated against and laughed at—all because they are fat.

Add to that the inescapable fact that every extra pound a person carries around is a health hazard, especially in adulthood when the obese individual will be many times more susceptible than a slim one to heart attacks, high blood pressure, diabetes, accidents, and arteriosclerosis.

That is why you must help your child grow up thin. That is why you must make up your mind to be strong and consistent, to truly believe that what you're about to do is right and that you're not depriving your child of anything but an unhappy future. It must and can be done. I know because I have helped parents slim down hundreds of overweight children.

And even if your school-age child has been relatively thin until now, I recommend listening carefully to what I am saying here. For reasons no one knows for sure, perhaps because their physical activity is now curtailed by sitting at a desk in school or sitting at home doing homework, many children begin to put on unwanted weight at around seven or eight.

The overweight youngster obviously eats too much of the wrong foods and exercises too little. That is what you're going to change—slowly and gradually. No growing child must be placed on a quickie crash diet nor must he take any medication whatsoever unless your pediatrician, after careful tests, has found a real need for it. It is exceedingly rare that there is a medical problem, a glandular deficiency. If there is, your doctor will know it and help you cope. If there isn't, pills and potions are emphatically out.

Let the Doctor Decide

I am not trying to drum up business, but I advise parents to take their school-age children, fat or thin, to their pediatrician *at least* once a year for a checkup. Most parents stick faithfully to checkup schedules while their children are small, then tend when they start school to see the doctor only when illness befalls them. Aside from other health advantages, regular visits will put your pediatrician in a position to know whether Jimmy or Susie is gaining weight too rapidly, before the situation becomes critical, and whether it's necessary to do something about it.

I find that I am often more concerned about weight than the parents of my patients. Perhaps that's because many people do not yet recognize that a child who is fat—at any age, but especially by the time she starts school—is likely to be fat at fourteen, at twenty and at forty-five. Slimming down to a normal weight is going to become more and more difficult as time goes by, and the psychological and physical damage is going to mount.

Don't Take the Easy Way Out

On the other hand, I see mothers every day who do worry about their overweight youngsters but somehow can't bring themselves to change their own habits. Mrs. S., the mother of a nine-year-old who came to my office recently, is a good example. She said, "Doctor Eden, I know John eats too much but he's always hungry and he loves sweets. I can't keep saying no to him. I say no and he begs until I give in. I hate to see him suffer, and it's so much easier to give in than fight with him all day long."

I tell all overindulgent "softhearted" parents that they are doing their children irreparable harm by following the easy route. I try to convince them—and I manage with some of them—that they must not feel guilty and defensive when they take a stand for what they know is right. Would they feel guilty if they refused to let their child cross the street in front of a large truck? Would they be apologetic for saying "no" when she insisted on touching the hot stove? Of course not. Though the damage comes more slowly than getting hit by a truck, it does come, emotionally now when she's the last to be chosen for the ball game because she can't run fast enough and physically later when she's the first on the block to have a heart attack.

Parents must be able to take the flak, from themselves and their persuasive children, if they're going to transform a fatty into a slim healthy child who won't spend her life hating what she looks like. They must take the responsibility, because a six-year-old or even an eleven-year-old child can't.

Out on Her Own

And now, with the lecture over, let's get down to the facts of life with a school-age youngster. When your child starts going to school all day, many things change. She is no longer under your complete control, her every moment supervised, her every mouthful monitored. She has schedules to meet, less time to herself. She is influenced by peers, schoolmates, teachers, whom you may not even know. She gets an allowance which she may usually dispose of as she pleases. She must discipline herself to effort, and to sitting in one place many hours a day. She travels around with her friends, out of your sight, venturing out into her own world which involves you less and less each year.

All of this, normal though it may be, can hinder your

efforts to help her grow up thin, and means more of a
struggle if she's already overweight.

Food, even if it has never been a problem before, often
becomes one now. In most households, school mornings
mean a tremendous rush, with breakfast bolted down on the
run so that everyone can be out the door in time to get to
school before the last bell rings. Sitting down to breakfast,
eating a well-balanced nutritious first meal, occurs only in
the most organized homes. I think it's most important that it
become a habit in your house, even if it means getting up a
half hour earlier in the mornings. Children need a good
energetic start in the morning, a start which will last them
till lunch.

What the School-Age Child Should Eat

The ideal breakfast for a school child consists of citrus fruit,
cold non-sugar-coated cereal or cooked cereal with only a
minimum of sugar sprinkled on top, perhaps a slice of toast,
skimmed milk, and some other kind of protein—maybe eggs
(though no more than three or four a week), or French
toast, bacon, ham, sausage, hamburger, cheese, or even nuts.
And to top it off, a multivitamin pill.

Not every child wants a big breakfast, and many aren't
used to being presented with one. But I suggest you make
an occasion out of breakfast. Let your youngster eat as much
or as little as she wants, but don't let her substitute
"quickie" foods which generally turn out to be chiefly sugar
or starch.

I recommend skimmed milk, by the way, for all children
of six or more to keep their cholesterol level down (see
Chapter 6 on nutrition). And I recommend that they
continue on skimmed milk from now on, whether they are
fat or thin.

During the morning at school, a child usually eats nothing, unless her school features junk-vending machines in the halls (in which case, protest vigorously to school authorities) or you've been foolish enough to send a snack along in her school bag. If she's had a nourishing breakfast, she'll be able to hold out till lunch.

The child who walks home from school for lunch not only gets some healthy exercise on the trip but also, hopefully, a proper lunch prepared by you or a nutritionally oriented stand-in.

Eating lunch in school is another story. If your child brown-bags it, taking lunch with her, don't give her jelly sandwiches and cookies. Prepare a protein sandwich, perhaps tuna fish or chicken, adding a leaf of lettuce or a slice of tomato. Include skimmed milk or fruit juice, a piece of fruit or perhaps some nuts for dessert. Resist tucking in those little surprise packages of potato chips, the can of soda, the lollipops.

If she buys lunch in the school cafeteria, you probably have a problem. Most schools offer disgraceful lunches, full of starch and sugar and high in calories. My son's favorite day used to be Wednesdays, when his school featured pizza slices and jelly doughnuts. There's not much you can do about the lunches sold in school except to try to influence your youngster to choose as well as possible, and to organize your fellow parents to press for better menu planning.

Leisurely Dinner Hours

Dinner is the one meal in many households bearing any real resemblance to planned nutrition. Ideally, as I've mentioned earlier, the whole family sits down to this meal together, eating at a leisurely pace, talking and sharing their days and their thoughts. The table is no place for battles, especially about food. No one should be pressured to eat, though, obviously, a well-balanced meal must be offered, with emphasis on protein, especially poultry and fish, and vegetables both green and yellow, and fruit. Desserts, unless they are fruit or cheese, are not desirable as a daily occurrence.

I suggest that one of the adults at the table dish out the food, rather than everyone helping himself. Portions for children should be small enough for them to finish easily, so the temptation to eat more than they want will be automatically eliminated. If they want seconds, let them request them and have them.

Allow your child to eat only as much as she wants, with no threats to send her to her room if she doesn't eat every bite, and no words of high praise if she licks her plate clean. Above all, don't offer a tasty goodie as a reward for eating dinner. Or, for that matter, as a reward for anything, including cleaning her room, quitting her temper tantrum, or being nice to Aunt Alice. Your ultimate aim is to teach a child to use food to satisfy her hunger, not her emotions.

Snacking Is a Way of Life

I doubt there's a child in America who doesn't consider a snack after school (and before dinner, after dinner, before bed, etc.) an inherent right. And I doubt there's an overweight eight-year-old who doesn't think an apple or a glass of skimmed milk an insult to her sensibilities and her stomach. Snacking, mainly on high-calorie food, is such a way of life today that many people, including children, rarely eat real meals but exist on nibbling all day long.

Snacking is such a concrete part of our existence that, apart from school hours, young children along with the rest of us seem to be constantly filling their mouths—and their fat cells. Home from school, it begins without delay. "I'm hungry, Mom. What have we got that's good?"

In your house, if you are concerned that your child grow up thin and strong and healthy, the snacks can't be junk food. They must be good body-building nutritious food which won't give her a lot of useless calories, poor teeth, excess fat tissue and bad habits which will remain with her forever. If you have not already done so, take fifteen to twenty minutes and fatproof your house, getting rid of all the unnecessary—and indeed harmful—trash foods. Those few minutes can be the most important time you will ever spend being a responsible parent.

Mothers often say to me, when I urge fatproofing on them, "But my kids aren't much overweight. Why shouldn't they have those things?" Because, fat or thin, those things aren't good for them. If your children are thin, they need food that builds bones and muscles. If they're overweight, they need to eliminate the enormous numbers of calories the junk food gives them.

Thinning Down the Overweight School Child

Suppose you have in your house right now a school-age child, say, eight or nine, who is far overweight. What would I recommend?

First of all, don't pick on her. She's eating too much because she's been allowed and probably encouraged to eat too much and to exercise too little. Shaming her, embarrassing her, isn't going to help at all and, in fact, it's going to hurt. She'll eat to get back at you or to smother her injured feelings. A fat child is already ashamed and embarrassed, for she probably lives with the taunts of her schoolmates every day. She knows she has to go to special shops to find clothes to fit and she worries about her lack of athletic abilities. She wants desperately to be thin and attractive. While boys may sometimes talk themselves into thinking fat is muscle, girls know for sure it isn't.

One little boy I know is referred to by most of his schoolmates as "the fat kid." There's a good chance that some day a psychiatrist will have to help straighten out this youngster's emotional problems.

The overweight eight-year-old daughter of some friends of mine flatly refused to go to school for over a week because some neighborhood children taunted her all the way to and from school every day. Talks with their parents put an end to the overt activity. The girl returned to school but, I assure you, not as the happiest student you could find.

Write It All Down

Before you begin my program, keep track for a while of what your child eats in a day to get an idea of how many calories she normally takes in. The best way is to write it all down, every bite. I recommended that to Mrs. H., the mother of one of my overweight patients, who adamantly maintained that her eleven-year-old Jennifer didn't eat very much. After a week, she called to report her amazement at the amount her child managed to stow away in a day—and, at that, she undoubtedly missed a few choice items consumed on side trips Jennifer made with her friends.

While making an effort to slim a child down, parents must be interested and encouraging and quite matter of fact. And they must be convinced in their own minds that they have a job to do. That job is to take the pressure off their overweight child and put it on themselves where it rightly belongs.

You're in Charge

It is the responsibility of the adults in your house, *you,* to select the food that's eaten there. Not your child and not the advertising industry, which does its best to get your children to eat their products. You have to change the eating habits of your household, buying and preparing food that's healthy and not loaded with calories. Don't put the burden of eating correctly on your child, constantly lecturing and admonishing, weighing and nagging her. Don't start counting calories or measuring portions.

Just take temptation out of her way. Quietly. Firmly. Consistently. Undefensively.

You have to believe me when I tell you that this works. In the families which have done as I've advised, success has been prompt and often fantastic. In those where the parents haven't been strong enough to resist the initial pressure, who have given up their prerogatives to their children, who have tried to make one child eat differently from the rest of the family, stay on a diet all alone, avoid certain foods in the house, nothing positive has been accomplished at all.

Stories of Two Families

I'll tell you two stories from my experience to illustrate my point. Tommy G. is ten years old and overweight. His thirteen-year-old brother, George, is what I call just right, while his parents consider him slightly emaciated. When I suggested that they fatproof their house, providing only healthy, nourishing, low-calorie foods to eat, they agreed they would do it, and they did. But a week hadn't gone by when Mrs. G. began to buy "a few little treats" for George, "because he really needs the weight." Soon the larder was stocked up pretty much as before, with Tommy consuming his fair share and continuing to be fat.

On the other hand, the T. family contained an exceedingly overweight ten-year-old girl, Darlene, along with two other children who were normal weight. Darlene and her mother were locked in constant battle over the food the child ate, with no good results whatsoever. In fact, I could see that the tension and resentment that had built up between the two was becoming a way of life.

After a long discussion, Mrs. T. promised to do things my way, though she was sure it wouldn't work. She cleaned out her house, got rid of all the undesirable (by my standards) food, and expected the worst.

For about two weeks, all three children badgered and pleaded, complained and demanded. But somehow Mrs. T. remained resolute. Soon the clamor ceased and, she told me, she couldn't believe how much better she and Darlene got along.

Now, six months later, the change is obvious and delightful. Darlene has lost five pounds, grown one inch, and is well on her way to her ideal weight. She and her mother have abandoned their old bickering routine and the other two children have not wasted away to nothing.

Fatproofing Works

With the vast majority of overweight children, the one act of fatproofing the house will do the job. It's as simple as that. If your child can't find a bite of junk food in the house where she spends most of her time outside of school, she obviously won't be snacking on it all day long. It's been shown that perhaps half of the calorie intake of the average American occurs outside of the regular three meals a day.

When the peanut clusters aren't in the candy dish, the rice chips aren't in the cupboard, the Cracker Jacks are gone from the shelf, and the cupcakes have vanished from the cake box, then a carrot stick, a piece of fruit, or a glass of juice is going to start looking pretty good.

"What's Going on Around This House?"

Obviously, you are going to have to explain to your overweight youngster what is suddenly going on around here. It will be traumatic at first and you'll be accused of being mean, cruel, and uncaring. But, if you stick to your guns, and don't make little exceptions every other day because you're afraid your child won't love you anymore, the complaining will cease. After a while, if you're consistent, the subject won't come up too often. And when it does, you now know what you're going to say—"Sorry, we don't eat that anymore at home. It's not healthy."

Children are smart—when they see they're not getting to you, they'll quit wasting their time. It's like dealing with a small baby who gets in the habit of crying every night wanting some attention. If her parents make sure all her needs are taken care of and then are strong enough to let her cry a bit without picking her up for a few nights, she'll start to sleep through.

Not only will you find your overweight youngster growing thinner from lack of junk foods consumed in the house, but you'll also discover there's less tension in the air. Eliminating the foods firmly and consistently answers the question, "Can I have a cookie?" There aren't any. You'll have cut out all that begging and nagging you get now after you've told your fat child she doesn't *need* any cookies.

Stick to Your Guns

I urge you not to hide the cookies and the candy and the other trash in a private cache where only you will know the location. Sooner or later, you'll be tempted to present just one to your child as a reward or to get her off your neck. Now she'll know you're vacillating, that she can always win if she keeps at you long enough.

Do your child a favor—make it clear that this kind of food isn't there and won't be, no matter how hard she begs. You'll be doing yourself a favor too. Your relationship will improve, and *you* won't be eating the junk either.

So, your overweight eight-year-old, home from school and proclaiming hunger, just isn't going to find the junk food in the house. No matter how much she whines and wails, it's not going to be there. She'll have to make do on fruit, or cheese, or skimmed milk or juice, or whole-wheat crackers, and she'll survive till dinnertime.

And at bedtime, when most children are accustomed to raiding the cookie jar, it's going to be empty. No cookies. How about an apple or a carrot stick that's all ready to eat and stored in a jar in the refrigerator?

Nothing "Worth Eating"

Many mothers tell me that the crunch comes when Johnny and Janie bring their friends home to play. The friends are astounded to discover there aren't any "good" snack foods in the house and they're faced with pears to eat. One mother of a very overweight boy told me she'd been doing very well at passing by the endless snack counters in the supermarket and heading straight for the fresh-food departments until her son one afternoon brought home a group of ravenous buddies who wouldn't believe there was nothing "worth eating" there.

Gripped by anxiety that the group would reject her boy and never come over to play again, she backed down. "Hold on for ten minutes, boys. I'll be back." And off she hurried to the store for the kind of supplies she knew would please them.

I agreed she had a problem, but I didn't agree with the way she handled it. I explained that she must expect this situation, anticipate it and be prepared, if she wants her child to lose weight. I said, "Tell the visitors that you don't eat those foods in your house and that's that. If they ask why, say you don't consider them healthy. They may think you're a bit queer, but I doubt if they'll turn against Bobby because of it." Offer them cheese and crackers, or fruit, or—if you must—diet soda.

Another mother told me the complaints came from her other child, fourteen and thin. To her I explained that the fourteen-year-old must be convinced that she has to be helpful. I told her to have a serious talk with the teen-ager (or I would if she preferred) and convince her that it wouldn't be fair for her to consume empty calories while her little sister watched. And besides, she could be skinny as a rail and not need junk foods.

Don't Be a Cop

Well, I'm then asked, what about the snacks Betsy eats outside the house? She visits her friends and their mothers distribute food. She has her allowance and she can easily spend it on sodas and candy. Everybody stops by McDonald's or Carvel now and then. That's true but I do not recommend being a policeman, and I do not suggest constant questioning about what she ate where. Ninety percent of the time, the child who is not tremendously overweight will slim down noticeably merely by the change in eating patterns in the house.

As for the child who has a lot of weight to lose, then you must try to convince her to take it easy when you're not around. With my patients, I find it helps for *me* to discuss the situation with them seriously and respectfully, and let their parents carry on from there.

I tell the youngsters the reasons they shouldn't go out with their pals for pizza and Coke too often, though once in a while is understandable, why they should try to pass the candy store by, and how to order a low-calorie soda and sugarless gum when their friends buy junk.

I explain why a stop at McDonald's, for example, shouldn't be a regular part of their trip home from school. (While there's a certain amount of nourishment in a Big Mac, for instance, it consists mainly of fat and starches, and a hefty 557 calories. Add to that a small order of french fries, 215 calories, and a chocolate milk shake, 317.)

If a child won't go along, the best I and her parents can do is to continue our plan at home, and hope that one day slimming down will be important enough to her to work at it. Let's not kid ourselves—the child of this age who is determined to eat will find a way. Some who are completely miserable because of their obesity refuse to make a conscious connection between food and fat. Or, like the rest of us, they will plan to start tomorrow. I see no point in continual nagging—when she reaches adolescence or maybe not until young adulthood, perhaps she will have enough motivation to make the effort to lose weight.

Occasionally the reward system will help give a school child the motivation she doesn't get merely from looking in the mirror. Obviously, the reward for slimming down can't be chocolate bars, though I've been amazed how many parents promise them, but an inedible something the child really covets. Maybe a new basketball, a new wardrobe, a bike, tickets to a show.

No Dieting Needed

Mothers always want to know, obviously, what to feed their overweight children at meals. My theory is that if the extra poundage is not too excessive, merely cutting out the constant snacking is probably the answer and meals don't have to change except for the elimination of rich desserts most of the time. It's very hard to eat enough meat, vegetables, fruit, or even potatoes to get fat.

But, if a child is more than a little fat and your pediatrician recommends more drastic action, then it pays to be somewhat restrictive at meals. Keep in mind that no child should lose weight rapidly as it can affect her eventual height. No child should go on a very strict diet, unless it is medically indicated and supervised.

I do not suggest you measure portions or count calories. Merely follow a few sensible rules.

Rules for Meal Makers

- Don't make too many starchy main dishes.
- Serve well-balanced meals (see Chapter 6) that include some form of protein (preferably poultry, veal or fish to keep your child's cholesterol level low), plenty of vegetables and fruit.
- Dish out the meals yourself, giving your child a moderate-sized first portion of everything, letting her come back for more if she wants, except of the starchy foods.
- Buy only the thin-sliced bread and restrict your

dangerous on city and many suburban streets. That physical activity usually requires the participation of the parents, who themselves have become accustomed to not doing much.

A school-age child who is going to slim down needs to get more exercise to burn up the food she takes in. The earlier you begin encouraging her to use her muscles, the more she will persist on her own.

Aside from letting her walk to school, walk to her friends' houses, walk to the store, instead of driving her (and yourself) wherever she's going, and give her chores to do around the house. Even taking the garbage out uses up calories; and vacuuming the rugs and washing the windows uses up more. She can make her bed, carry laundry up from the basement, run to the hardware store, help you rake the lawn, fetch your book from the bedroom.

Do It Together

I have found that children usually fare best in families that pursue physical activity as a group. When everyone sets off to swim or bowl or skate or jog, when the whole family takes a week skiing in the mountains, or makes a habit of hiking through the woods looking for chipmunks, it's not only fun, it uses up calories, and it gives everyone more to talk about together besides.

Concern yourself with the physical-education programs at the school. Get other parents interested in visiting the school with you to be sure the program provides at least an hour of physical activity every day no matter what the weather, plus organized after-school sports for girls as well as boys.

Arrange for your child to start learning a carry-over sport, a sport she can continue to play the rest of her

life—like swimming, tennis, skating, bowling, biking. I
started playing tennis when I was ten—and I'm an ardent
player today. I also was a big baseball player as a kid—but
the chances of getting up a game as an adult are very slim. If
a child learns a skill now, she'll be proficient enough by the
time she's an adolescent to want to continue. If you wait, it
won't be easy to push a reluctant teen-ager into action.

Sherry Gets Tired

A mother came into my office one day, ostensibly for a
checkup for her fat nine-year-old daughter. After I'd looked
the child over thoroughly and found no problems, I made a
strenuous effort to motivate both the mother and the child to
work on her weight. Neither seemed interested. Then the
mother, markedly overweight herself, said to me, "Doctor, I
wonder if you'd give us a note stating that Sherry's
classroom should be changed. Her classroom is on the third
floor and the poor child has to walk up and down two flights
of steps three times a day. It's too much for her."

"I don't see why it's too much for her," I said. "What's
the problem?"

"Well, she gets very tired."

I didn't write the note. In fact, I told them that, judging
from everything I could see, Sherry was very lucky she had
those two flights of stairs to climb every day. It seemed to
me it was the only exercise she ever had.

I constantly get requests, too, for notes to the school
nurse asking her to excuse certain children from gym class.
Why? Because Marcia's had a little cold all week, Jimmy's
not feeling up to par, and Edna gets tired very easily.
Usually it's a fat child who asks for notes, because many of
them are embarrassed to undress in front of the other kids.
But these are the youngsters who need the exercise the

most. Unless I see a real reason for a child to skip gym, she doesn't get any notes from me. In fact, these are the times when I usually give my speech about the need for more exercise, not less.

If food is not to turn to blubber, activity must burn it up. Consider that a glass of cola contains about 95 calories. For the inactive child, 95 calories (along with 185 for a slice of pizza, 520 for a large chocolate milk shake) will stay with her, signing on as fat. But she could burn up the calories from the cola in five minutes of running or thirteen minutes of bike riding, and the ice-cream soda in a half hour of running.

Jean Mayer has written: "In a program conducted by our research group in a large public school system . . . several hundred obese children and adolescents lost weight and kept it off for several years while the program was in effect. This was achieved essentially through stepped-up daily physical activity, although they were also given thorough instruction in nutrition and received psychological support. . . . They were given daily physical education in special classes and directed as to exercising on their own during weekends and holidays.

"The great majority improved steadily under this regimen, particularly those who were taken in hand in the first elementary grades."

Waiting for Miracles?

I don't doubt that you, reading this book, agree with me that our children's habits have to change, from overconsumption and underexertion to healthy eating and exercise.

I don't doubt that you object in some ways to our current affluent and sedentary life and feel some nostalgia for certain aspects of "hard times."

Maybe you even agree with me that it's disgraceful that our children are getting fatter, less coordinated, less active, more prone to debilitating diseases when they grow up.

If you do, then you can't wait for miracles, you must get going on changing those habits, that fat. The time to begin is *now* so that your children can avoid the tremendous problems of adolescent obesity. You can catch up with fat anytime, but it becomes harder to fight every year. Do your children an invaluable service by keeping them thin.

If your child is about to enter adolescence, check the risk scoring table for age twelve to see how she stands. Low risk? Great. Chances are obesity will never be one of her problems. Moderate risk? Not so good. You had better get busy. High risk? This is real trouble. But it still is not too late to lower the risk. If you are able to slim your child down through adolescence, she may end up in the moderate-risk category, with a much better chance to remain thin as an adult.

12

How to Cope with an Overweight Adolescent—Don't!

Scoring the Risk at 12 Years

One fat parent . . . . 2 points
Two fat parents . . . . 4 points
Fat at 1 year . . . . 2 points
Fat at 2 years . . . . 2 points
Fat at 6 years . . . . 2 points
Fat at 10 years . . . . 2 points
Fat at 12 years . . . . 2 points

Your child's total . . . . _____

0–4 points makes him a low risk for becoming a fat adult.
6–10 points makes him a moderate risk.
12–14 points makes him a high risk.

I have two words of advice for parents of overweight adolescents: *bug off*. I've worked many years with fat teen-agers and I've found through bitter experience that the less said or done by you about your adolescent youngster's need to lose weight, the better.

Your role must be an almost passive one, providing

Scoring the Risk at 14 Years

One fat parent .... 2 points
Two fat parents .... 4 points
Fat at 1 year .... 2 points
Fat at 2 years .... 2 points
Fat at 6 years .... 2 points
Fat at 10 years .... 2 points
Fat at 12 years .... 2 points
Fat at 14 years .... 2 points

Your child's total .... _____

0–4 points makes him a low risk for future
  fat.
6–10 points makes him a moderate risk.
12–16 points makes him a high risk.

Scoring the Risk at 16–18 Years

One fat parent .... 2 points
Two fat parents .... 4 points
Fat at 1 year .... 2 points
Fat at 2 years .... 2 points
Fat at 6 years .... 2 points
Fat at 10 years .... 2 points
Fat at 12 years .... 2 points
Fat at 14 years .... 2 points
Fat at 16–18 years .... 2 points

Your child's total .... _____

0–4 points makes him a low risk of being a
  fat adult.
6–12 points makes him a moderate risk.
14–18 points makes him a high risk.

encouragement *when* and *if* there's some success, discussion and advice *if* it's wanted, a lot of sympathy and support for a job that's very hard, *plus* a kitchen that contains only the right foods.

This is because, in this adolescent period that's filled with frustrations and fears and questions, the truth is that parents who push and pressure, pester, restrict, embarrass, punish, and nag, even parents who merely remind, usually have the worst results. It's as simple as that.

Cool It, or Else

So, cool it. Don't be an active partner in this enterprise. Don't monitor every bite your child puts in his mouth. Don't watch him weigh himself. Don't ask him what he weighs this week. Don't count calories for him. If you become overinvolved, I think you'll see the usual result—rebellion. It's almost as if whatever you say right now, your adolescent will take the opposite position because he's got to show he's on his own. Sometimes I think if parents would say, "I want you to gain weight," just for spite their youngsters would go on a diet. Besides, the teen years are the time of growing independence and self-reliance. A youngster's own weight can surely be one problem we can permit him to deal with without interference from parents.

An estimated 10 to 25 percent of American adolescents are overweight. The majority of them are girls whose changing metabolism promotes the deposit of fat more than that of boys and whose concern about their configurations is much more intense as well.

Girls, throughout their lives, always have a greater percentage of fat tissue, which increases proportionately as they grow, than boys of the same height and age. That is why girls have a greater tendency to be overweight and need fewer calories for growth as well as weight stabilization.

A Tough Time to Lose

Most experts agree that adolescence is probably the most difficult period in an entire lifetime in which to lose weight because, as the National Institutes of Health reports, "the entire physiology of the adolescent is geared to promote growth, and any attempt to reverse any of its growth parameters may be met with insuperable resistance." If you add to that the psychological resistance of a teen-ager to advice from his elders, especially his parents, you can see that reversing the trend at this stage is not easy.

That is why it is generally agreed that avoiding overweight from the beginning of a child's life, rather than trying to deal with it at this age, is much the best idea. Fat rarely has its beginnings in adolescence but usually reflects a fat family, a fat childhood, and eating and exercising habits that have become firmly established through the years. Research by the University of Washington's Adolescent Clinic, though, shows that parents often fail to become concerned about a child's obvious weight problem until he reaches puberty.

And, says Dr. S. L. Hammar, director of medical services and training at Kauikeolani Children's Hospital in Hawaii, "In our experience there is often a long delay in seeking professional help. . . . It is only when the psychosocial problems become distressingly obvious to the parents, the school, or the public health nurse" that help is sought.

Preadolescent Puppy Fat

Immediately preceding adolescence, in the period called prepuberty, most children, girls in particular, seem to be preparing for the coming rapid growth spurt, their subcutaneous fat increasing appreciably.

As Dr. William A. Daniel, author of *The Adolescent Patient*, says, "Almost all eleven- or twelve-year-old children with adequate food available to them are plump." While some "puppy fat" is normal, it's important that it not get out of hand because this is a time of rapid multiplication of the body's fat cells. If these increase in number too quickly, much more quickly than the norm, the youngster will end up (even if he hasn't been overweight before) with a collection of excess cells that will never leave him. In other words, this overweight preadolescent will have a higher-than-normal risk of being fat all his life.

If an overweight *pre*adolescent then becomes a fat *adolescent*, his chances of a thin future become even smaller. (See the scoring at the head of the chapter for your child's chances of forever fighting fat.) For children who have always been overweight, weight loss now is especially crucial so that they do not continue to overproduce fat cells. They will, admittedly, have a harder time accomplishing it than youngsters who were thin children and only now have become too heavy, because they may have genes which predispose them to fat, their fat cells are already more numerous than a previously thin child, and their eating and exercise habits are thoroughly ingrained.

All that understood, it *is* possible for your overweight adolescent youngster to slim down now. It won't be as easy as it might have been at an earlier age, but it *can* be done.

What's more, it can be done without "diets" and without "suffering," if you follow my plan.

As you surely know by now, I do not recommend "diets" for children, and that includes teen-agers. I do not recommend counting calories either, though some knowledge of what kinds of foods contain more calories than others, and how much activity burns them up, is certainly a good idea.

My non-diet has helped hundreds of my patients stop gaining weight and make the switch from fat to thin. All I require is that they follow a few "don'ts." A smaller list of "do's." And that they weigh themselves once a week.

Teen-agers are impatient people and, like the rest of us, have little follow-through. They look for miracles and, also like the rest of us, fall for "magic pills," injections, fad diets. They want to wake up thin tomorrow morning. I don't blame them and I certainly sympathize, but if these methods are ever a good idea—and I don't believe they are—they are certainly not a good idea now while growth is still going on.

No Pills or Fad Diets

First of all, no diet pills and no injections—they are dangerous. No thyroid pills. It is an extremely rare child or adolescent who suffers from glandular disturbances—the "sluggish" thyroid, so long blamed for fat, is *rarely* the culprit. Your pediatrician can find out through tests if your child is the exception. Before you accept *any* prescription for *any* medication designed to help your youngster lose weight, including hormones, make *sure* he has been given the proper testing for any possible deficiencies.

Fad diets, though they promise miracles, don't work in the long run. Most of the dramatic loss is water, not fat, and promptly returns when the youngster begins to eat normally. Besides, it's a rare person who can stay with a peculiar diet for a long enough time to see real results.

Most important, rapid weight loss can be hazardous for an

adolescent. If his diet is so restricted that he begins to use up his body's store of protein, his growth can be reduced or even stopped altogether. I remember the case of one family with two obese parents and a markedly overweight child. At the age of thirteen, without proper medical supervision, the boy went on a very restrictive diet. He lost an enormous amount of weight in a short time but, unfortunately, in addition to being thin, he ended up very short.

The right way is for teen-agers to *slow down—or stop—the rate of gain.* As they grow taller and broader, they will then become thinner. Their muscle and bone and other tissues will make up a larger proportion of their bodies while their percentage of body fat will decrease. The scales may not change much but they will *look* very different.

To stop or slow down the rate of gain, very little has to happen. A tiny adjustment in calorie intake or energy expenditure, perhaps only 100 calories a day, will do it. A hundred fewer calories a day (one can of soda, perhaps, or about ten minutes of vigorous bike riding) amounts to ten pounds worth of weight in a year.

Even when a youngster is extremely overweight, and some actual weight *loss* is recommended, that loss must be slow and gradual, a maximum of one pound a week. That's not out of sight either, when you consider that 500 calories (one malted milk shake or an hour of bike riding) a day is worth a pound a week. A pound a week adds up to fifty-two pounds in a year. If you add that actual loss to the inches a teen-ager grows in that year, it equals even more.

Right now, I want to talk to *you,* the *parents* of an overweight adolescent. In the next chapter, I'll have a talk with the kids. I want to explain some facts of a fat life to you, tell you how you can help your child, and try to convince you to hand the responsibility for losing weight over to him—and to me.

Adolescence Is a Time of Change

Adolescence is a period of fantastic growth, a time when a youngster changes faster than he has since his first year of life. From the ages of ten to eighteen, he doubles his body mass, his body metamorphosing into that of an adult.

Until about ten, boys and girls grow at similar rates. According to the U.S. Public Health Service's National Institutes of Health, "The typical girl in the U.S. now begins puberty at the age of ten and a half. For the next two and a half years, she grows at an average annual rate of three inches per year. With the onset of the menstrual cycle, about age thirteen, the adolescent girl then experiences a rapid decline in growth rate but will continue to grow, at a reduced pace, for another three years. By the age of sixteen . . . further increase in height is [usually] impossible.

"The average adolescent boy, on the other hand, is [usually] only beginning his growth spurt at age thirteen. It will usually be more marked, more intense, and of longer duration than that of the girl. . . . For example, during the next two and a half years . . . the adolescent boy usually grows at least four inches a year. By the time he is fifteen, he will be eating seven times more protein and 50 percent more calories than he consumed at age nine . . . his increase in height is not over until he reaches his late teens."

The very fat child, however, tends to reach puberty earlier than other children, growing taller sooner as well, though his eventual height averages out about the same or even a little shorter.

Emotionally, as every parent finds out, adolescence is a difficult time for everyone in the family as their child adjusts to a new body, ready or not. As the father of two teen-agers, as well as a pediatrician involved with many adolescents, I can tell you that this period of transition is not easy for the parents or for the youngsters.

The *overweight* adolescent has an especially rough time. He is a fat person in a thin world at a time when being accepted by his peers is the most important thing in his life. Add to that the constant dieting, the frequent difficulty in finding attractive clothing that fits, the preoccupation with appearance, the inevitable erosion of self-esteem and self-confidence, the real and imagined rejections. Tack on the normal emotional turmoil of growing up, as well as the early puberty, and the sum has to come out total misery.

Fat Isn't Fun

Fat kids hate to be fat. They feel ashamed, depressed and ineffective. They have a very low regard for themselves and their capabilities. They are positive something is wrong with them because they are different from the other kids. They feel rejected—and often they are. And the longer they stay heavy, the worse the feelings become. According to one study of obese adolescent girls, these young people proved to be psychologically similar to ethnic and racial minorities, very sensitive to and preoccupied by their position in society. Burdened by feelings of isolation and unacceptability, they blamed themselves for their condition and their condition for all of their problems.

Overweight girls are even more distressed by their bodies than obese boys, usually intensely disliking what they see in the mirror and often obsessed with their fat and their feelings of inferiority and social rejection. Boys, unless they are tremendously overweight, usually think of themselves as big and strong and are less worried about what other people think of them.

Parents cannot lose weight for an adolescent. During the early years, it's possible for you to have absolute control over what your child eats. As a child grows older, this gradually becomes less and less feasible. By the time he is about twelve, and certainly thereafter, the motivation for slimming down *must* come from him. You can't inject him with your own. You can't *put* him on a diet and expect results.

Put yourself in his place for a minute. A fat adolescent is usually miserable about being fat. He's desperately anxious to lose weight. So you don't have to convince him how important it is—he knows. The question is, how can it be done?

If you push and nag and he can't make it, you'll only have added to his unhappiness with himself. One girl I saw in my office recently summed it up when she said to me, "I know I look awful. I know I should lose weight and I try. I can't stand it when my mother starts talking about it because she looks so disappointed about having a daughter like me."

The worst thing parents can do is to attempt to shame or embarrass a youngster into losing weight. He feels bad enough. He's not happy about his body either. So I advise you, don't get personal. Don't use shock therapy. It won't work and it will depress your teen-ager even more.

Mrs. R. came to my office with her fourteen-year-old daughter a few months ago and said to me, "Doctor, I don't know why she's like that. I've always been careful about my weight. Look at her, she's a blimp. Look at those rolls of fat. It's really disgusting. What are we going to do about it?"

As her mother carried on, Susan sat there, eyes down, the most miserable-looking person I'd ever seen.

I told Mrs. R. she'd said enough. She was not to mention the subject to her daughter again, but to leave the matter up to me. Susan and I would work together on the problem.

Mrs. R. was an extreme case but it's true that most

parents feel anger and frustration when their children are fat. They feel it's a reflection on them, on their upbringing, discipline and influence. And they feel guilty, that they must have done everything wrong if this is the result—a child who's fat.

I've spent a great deal of time trying to convince parents that preoccupation and overinvolvement aren't going to help their child lose weight. But acceptance of the youngster, fat or thin, and quiet encouragement might. It isn't necessarily the parents' fault their child is fat, and it certainly isn't the child's. He may well have been genetically predisposed to overweight (are either of you, his parents, overweight?), making its control difficult for everyone. He may have been overfed early in his life because it was the style then to have fat babies and thought to be a measure of good health. He may be following your example, if you are overweight, doing what you *do,* not what you *say.* You may have encouraged him to overeat by not recognizing he was becoming too heavy because that would mean recognizing your own problem.

Whatever the reasons for the situation, the time is *now.* And now is when we must try to help without blaming yourself or your child for past history.

Who Should *Help a Teen-ager Slim Down?*

If parents should not become overinvolved in their youngster's weight problem, who should help him? Somebody else. Someone who isn't emotionally involved. Someone who won't take progress or lack of progress personally. Someone who won't hassle him over every bite he eats. If you haven't a doctor who specializes in adolescent health, then let me be your advisor. I'll take you off the hook, work with your teen-ager, and be the third party you need.

Your Job Is Easy

Once you've decided to disengage yourself from the day-to-day fray, given up the constant supervision and the daily decisions about what your child should or shouldn't eat, you have only a few things to do.

Here's What You Do

Take your youngster to your doctor, preferably a reputable pediatrician, to whom teen-agers seldom repair, having long since given up regular checkups (a mistake, especially when there's a weight problem). Let the physician check him out, make sure he has no physical problems affecting his weight. Do not accept medications or pills unless all proper tests have been made. Unfortunately, some doctors take the easy way out. If the doctor is willing to work with your youngster, let them confer privately, hopefully at regular intervals. This is between the two of them. If the doctor doesn't seem cooperative, I suggest trying to find another who is willing to deal with an overweight teen-ager sympathetically. In some large communities, you can find helpful adolescent clinics as well.

Second, be sure there's an accurate scale in the house.

Next, you must fatproof the house. I've discussed fatproofing throughout this book, but it is especially important now because teen-agers have tremendous appetites. Eliminate *all* the junk foods (those with little nourishment and many calories) from your house. All the sodas, cookies, potato chips, ice cream, sugar-coated cereals, candy, etc. All of it.

Throw it out. Give it away. And don't keep a secret cache in the back of the closet for special occasions.

Most junk foods appear in the attractive form of between-meal snacks and are what usually put on and provide the upkeep for unwanted pounds. It's hard to eat enough at mealtimes to get fat, unless you eat nothing but cream of mushroom soup, macaroni and cheese, french fries, and spaghetti. But it is easy to devour enough snacks to add up to a tremendous number of unused calories which will be cozily stored in the fat cells.

Consider that a two-inch piece of chocolate cake with chocolate icing contains 345 calories, a malted milk shake 520, a bottle of cola 145, three medium-sized caramels 115, chocolate pudding 385, and a small six-ounce chocolate bar 900; a cup of vanilla fudge ice cream 275, six chocolate-chip cookies 300, and the same number of chocolate-covered marshmallow cookies an astronomical 840.

Get rid of it all. If you buy or make calorie-laden desserts, which is quite acceptable *occasionally*, have only enough for that single meal. Never keep it in your house where it can be used for a quick snack.

Instead, for snacking, provide plenty of fresh fruit, raw vegetables, hard cheeses. For treats, buy low-calorie sodas and perhaps diet gelatin desserts. Nothing else. Substitute skimmed milk for whole milk—many adolescents drink enormous quantities of milk.

Do not count calories and don't get involved with the ritual of weighing. Cut the comments. Simply clear the shelves of junk. And don't replenish it no matter how much pressure you get. If it's there, your fat adolescent will eat it—he won't leave it for his thin sister—so it can't be there. If he wants it, he'll have to walk to the store to get it.

You're All in This Together

Naturally, there are going to be complaints from everybody, including the father of the house. "What about the rest of us? Do we all have to suffer for the sake of one?"

My answer to that is, "Yes, and I don't consider it suffering." Nobody, fat or thin, parent or child, needs junk food and if they must have it, let them eat it outside the house. As with other age groups we've discussed earlier, without the whole family's cooperation this plan is not going to work because it takes an unusually strong-willed youngster to resist what's there in the kitchen cabinet or on the refrigerator shelf.

I have a friend, Charlie, who is slim, as is his wife. Their adolescent daughter, Elsie, is quite plump, which distresses everyone in the family as they are a weight-conscious group. Elsie tries hard to lose weight but hasn't been successful. We were discussing this one evening and her father said, "She insists on having a big piece of cake every night. She says she's watching what she eats but she can't resist the cake."

"That's funny," I said. "What's the cake doing there?"

"Charlie has to have a piece of his favorite cake before he goes to bed at night," his wife explained. "It's a ritual."

"Well," I answered, "he's just going to have to do without it. It's got to go. Either that, or leave Elsie alone. Let her be fat." Charlie was horrified—no cake? But when the shock wore off, he agreed to forego it and so did Elsie.

Many fat and unhappy adolescents (as well as fat and unhappy adults) are binge eaters. When they are depressed, as they frequently are, they eat, usually consuming enormous amounts of high-calorie food. Then, even unhappier because of what they've done, they eat more. One sixteen-year-old girl came to my office recently to discuss her weight problem. After a long talk, she confessed to me that she was a binge eater. During the week, while she was busy at school, everything was fine. But on weekends, when her girlfriends were out "having fun," she sat at home eating cookies and candy. Where did the cookies and candy come from? Her mother kept a supply always at hand.

I told my young patient, after we'd discussed ways for her to lose weight, that I would have a talk with her mother so that the house would hopefully be fatproofed, taking the terrible temptations out of her way.

Outside Eating

Your next questions are sure to be: What about the junk foods my adolescent eats when he's not home? And, what if he brings the stuff home?

The answer: there's absolutely nothing at all you can do about the food your child eats outside the house. Teen-agers spend a good deal of their time floating around outside your sphere of influence, they have their own money, they can buy what they want. They can eat junk stocked by their friends' mothers too.

If your youngster wants to eat junk food, he can do it, and no amount of nagging on your part will stop him. He will quit, or cut down, *only* if he has enough determination to get thin. And if he hasn't, I'm sorry to say, that's the end of the story. Maybe he'll be ready to give it all up later when he's more mature.

If he brings food home, ignore it. Don't shout, "I want that stuff out of my house right now!" Don't take away his allowance. Don't check his pockets for candy wrappers. Your conscience is clear if you have cleared the house. Your job is done. From there on, it's his problem.

But if no trash food is available in the house (and your child is motivated enough not to go too wild outside), you'll be surprised at the results. Your youngster can't help but consume fewer calories each day and after a while, sitting in front of the TV set chewing on a carrot stick will seem *almost* as good as polishing off a box of pretzels. Very gradually, which is the way we want it, he will become longer and leaner.

Make a Habit of Serving Three Meals a Day

Your next job, as parents of a fat adolescent, is to change the way you eat in your house. By eliminating junk foods, you've made the first step. Now try to serve your family three distinct meals a day, as often as possible sitting down to the table together as a family.

With few exceptions, adolescents, particularly those with weight problems, skip breakfast entirely or have only a token meal. Starving by mid-morning, they fill up on candy bars or potato chips from the vending machines that line the school corridors. They eat lunch on the run, brown-bagged or purchased in the school cafeteria, and usually consisting of starch finished off by sweets. In the evening, they may take time out for the only occasion of the day that comes anywhere close to a real meal—dinner—which may be a ten-minute affair sandwiched between after-school activities and snacks and television and snacks.

Between meals, what the typical teen-ager eats boggles the mind. Junk food, topped off by more junk food. From the time dinner is over till they go to sleep, many adolescents go on a nonstop eating binge.

Adolescents consume tremendous numbers of calories, one estimate being between 3,500 and 4,000 a day. The truth is, they *need* more food now in order to fuel their rapid growth. The difficulty lies in knowing when and how to stop, and what *kinds* of food to eat.

Teen-agers, as a group, are the unhealthiest eaters in our entire population; many of them are actually undernourished despite a superabundance of food. *Fat* teen-agers often have the very worst eating habits, eating poorer quality food at less regular intervals than other people and usually outside of conventional meal hours. Research by the University of Washington's Adolescent Clinic revealed that the fat youngsters studied rarely had three meals a day. In addition, "the obese group revealed less structure around the eating situation" than the control group, some rarely eating with the family and others eating together but with a minimum of conversation and a maximum of television.

If you get up in the morning early enough to prepare a well-balanced breakfast for your children, you'll have gone a long way toward providing them with good nutrition, energy, and less need to stuff themselves with junk foods. According to Dr. R. E. Bennett of Austin, Texas, speaking to a 1974 symposium on overweight in Las Vegas, "The great percentage of overweight people skip breakfast. They eat one big meal a day, after their day's activities are finished, and they retain more. . . . You put gas in your car before you use it. You should fuel your body before you use it." Rather than letting them go off to school with no breakfast, or two sugar-coated Danishes washed down by a sweet fruit drink (one boy I know drinks cola in the morning), serve them food that will fend off their premonitions of starvation until it's time for lunch. See the chapter on nutrition for a list of the foods your teen-age child should consume every day.

Help your teen-ager pack a nourishing lunch to eat in school—perhaps a sandwich made of some kind of protein on thin-sliced bread. Fruit, raw vegetables, skimmed milk, or low-calorie soda.

It's been clearly demonstrated by research that cholesterol deposits (fatty plaques that can eventually clog the arteries) begin to be already apparent in adolescence. While these have no direct relationship with weight problems, they may affect your child's health later in his life. That's why I suggest thinking about cholesterol now, serving no more than three to four eggs a week, putting more emphasis than most of us do on veal, chicken, turkey and fish, using polyunsaturated cooking oil (read the label before you buy) and margarine, and, of course, serving skimmed milk.

I also suggest using the minimum amount of salt in cooking, and discouraging sprinkling salt over everything before it's even tasted. It can't be emphasized too strongly that too much salt can lead to high blood pressure and then to heart disease and kidney difficulties.

Dinner—a Family Ritual

Dinners, as often as humanly possible, should be eaten together with the rest of the family. Sometimes basketball practice or play rehearsals will interfere, but, as I've stressed earlier, suppertime should normally be a family ritual, with plenty of time to sit around the table talking, chewing, and digesting at leisure. No arguing, no tension.

Try to slow the meals down, serving the food in separate courses, with a short time between them. Fat people tend to eat very quickly, looking neither to right nor left, gobbling down unchewed food, eating much more than their stomachs demand. If one eats more slowly, the food becomes more satisfying.

Don't worry about portions. There's no way for an adolescent to take in the number of calories needed to make him fat by eating large amounts of nutritious foods—meats, fish, fruit, vegetables, even potatoes and pasta if they aren't served too often and he doesn't overdo the butter, sour cream, and sauces. But serve the meals yourself, dishing out moderate portions and then giving seconds, except of the starches, if they're requested. Your teen-ager won't feel deprived, because he's not on a *diet*.

A few don'ts (which I will explain to your teen-ager): Don't serve any beverages with meals except skimmed milk, low-calorie soda, tomato juice or water. Skip the desserts except for raw fruit, hard cheese or diet gelatin, except upon occasion. Don't serve bread at dinner.

Don't sit down to dinner early. Supper at 5:30 or 6:00 or even 6:30 leaves a lot of time till bedtime, bringing with it the "need" for snacking in the evening. On the other hand, a very late dinner can cause a lot of predinner snacking. You'll have to work out the best time for your family.

When everyone in the family eats together, everyone must eat the same way. Father can't have a Coke, and little sister can't have a piece of pecan pie. It's unfair to expect one member of the group to resist temptation. The only way you can truly influence your youngster to eat properly is to do the same yourself. It's like smoking. You cannot realistically expect your teen-ager not to smoke if you smoke yourself (as I learned, so I quit!). Lectures won't work. But examples can.

Overweight Teen-Agers Rarely Move

Your other major job as the parent of an overweight adolescent is to encourage him to get more exercise. Most of us assume that all teen-agers are physically busy, but studies have found that fat youngsters are decidedly less active than their thin counterparts. Many obese teen-agers, in fact, actually *eat less* than thin children, with their inactivity accounting for the calories which settle in as fat.

Harvard's Dr. Jean Mayer has done extensive research on exercise in relation to overweight. He asserts that lack of exercise is probably the most important single factor in the development of obesity in adolescents. "Energy balance," he says, "is determined as much by caloric output as by caloric intake. The range of daily caloric output in adolescent boys may go from 2,800 calories for the extremely inactive to over 6,000 for athletic young men engaged in strenuous sports."

Dr. Mayer and his colleagues studied the activity of groups of adolescent girls at summer camps, taking movies of them as they played volleyball and tennis and swam. It was found that the fat girls hardly moved at all. While their thin friends chased the tennis ball all over the court, the fat ones stood in one place and swung at the ball if it happened to come near them. While the thin girls thrashed through the water in the pool, the fat ones floated around, now and then taking a stroke or two.

In another research project, comparing an obese group of high-school girls with a thin group, Dr. Mayer found that "the time spent by the obese group in any sports or any sort of exercise was *less than half* that spent by the thin girls, the difference being absorbed by 'sitting' activities. . . . It appeared that for this particular group . . . inactivity was of greater importance than was overeating in the development of obesity." These high-school girls, both obese and non-obese, attended summer camp each year; almost without exception the enforced strenuous activity caused loss of weight despite simultaneously increased food intake.

It's hard to know which comes first, the fat or the immobility. Youngsters who don't exercise enough gain too much weight, while fat youngsters don't feel much like moving. It takes too much effort, it's hard to be graceful, and clumsiness is embarrassing. I couldn't count the number of tubby teen-agers, especially girls, who desperately ask me to help them get excused from gym class.

Whichever came first, it is most important to get

overweight adolescents to use their muscles and burn up calories. Don't drive your youngsters everywhere; as I have urged in regard to younger children, let your teen-agers walk or ride their bikes. An hour of brisk walking can get rid of 350 calories that would otherwise have turned to fat. Rather than push your child to do a half hour of exercises every day, which, to my knowledge, rarely works for long because it grows boring, encourage him to ride his bike (an hour uses up about 500 calories), jog (450 calories), take up sports that don't require vast numbers of teammates and can be played the rest of their lives. Perhaps you can find some activity that the entire family can enjoy together—like bowling, swimming, hiking or climbing.

As with eating, I advise you not to mercilessly nag your overweight adolescent to get moving. All you can do is suggest, encourage, provide the needed equipment and example, and then leave it up to him.

When he finds himself eager enough, motivated enough, to make the effort (and that, let's face it, may not be until he is more mature), he'll do it. In the meantime, all you'll accomplish by nagging and pushing is to generate more resistance, make him more unhappy, and frazzle your own nerves even further.

If your teen-ager seems truly interested in slimming down, suggest he read the next chapter.

13

For Teen-agers Only

If you're reading this only because your mother forced you to, you might as well not bother because it won't do either of us a bit of good. If, on the other hand, you're here because you honestly feel you are overweight, you don't like being so heavy, and you want to do something about it *yourself*, then stick with me. Maybe I can help.

Up till now, I've been talking to parents, but now I'd like to have a talk with you. To tell the truth, the less we involve your parents in your weight problems, the better off we'll be. You're no longer a little child and they can't possibly monitor every move you make and every bite you eat. So this is *your* problem, not theirs, and I've told them just that in the last chapter.

If you agree, let's discuss the problem of fat between the two of us and see if we can figure out possible solutions to it.

What I'm Not Going to Do

First, let me tell you what I'm *not* going to do.

I'm not going to tell you how to lose twenty pounds in

two weeks, or even in a month, so don't count on me for another "miracle" diet.

I'm not asking you to count calories.

I'm not giving you portion measurements.

I'm not telling you an apple will ever taste better than a Yankee Doodle.

And I'm not asking you to go hungry.

What I Am Going to Do

What *am* I going to do? I'm offering you a "non-diet" that will help you lose weight slowly and steadily, lowering the percentage of fat tissue in your body, so you'll never have to go through this again. I'm asking you to weigh yourself once a week, no more. I'm giving you a short list of "don'ts" and a shorter list of "do's." I've asked your parents to stock the house with certain foods and to clear it of others—and then to lay off and leave the rest to us.

Before I get to the specifics, I'd like to discuss a few basics with you, such as the following.

Do You Need to Lose Weight?

When you look in the mirror, are you happy with what you see? Are you really too fat? In my experience, many adolescents who really aren't at all overweight, or maybe only a little, are hooked on the idea of turning into a rail. And many who are truly fat don't see themselves that way.

Even your parents, though perhaps more knowledgeable than you, may not be good judges of your weight. Maybe too heavy themselves, they may think of you as "sturdy" or "healthy" or "pleasingly plump," rather than too fat. Or, if they're overly weight-conscious, they may think you're too fat when you're perfectly normal for your height and body build.

I think the best idea is to go to your doctor, preferably a pediatrician who deals with adolescents, and let him (her) tell you if you need to thin down. He or she sees many other teen-agers with problems similar to yours and on the basis of that and his (her) medical know-how is the person best equipped to make such an evaluation.

Why Lose Weight?

If you are truly and markedly overweight, I can tell you as a doctor that there's no question it's unhealthy. If you stay that way, you're going to be more susceptible to very serious diseases, like heart disease, high blood pressure, diabetes, kidney problems, and will probably die earlier than you would if you were thin. And you'll probably have more accidents, too, as fat people tend to be accident-prone.

Of course, besides health (which you may not be worrying about now), there are many other good reasons for losing weight which I'm sure you know better than I do. The social problems, for example: feelings of being rejected, left out; the fear of being laughed at; the fact that you can't move as fast as the others; the problem of finding attractive clothes that fit.

It's very unfair, but studies have shown that if you're interested in going to college and are still overweight then, you're less likely to be accepted than your thin friends who have exactly the same grades. And when you finish school, you'll find it harder to get a job even though you are just as competent as the other contenders.

Unfortunately, that's the way it is. People are prejudiced

against fat, and your life will be happier and healthier if you're not overweight.

What Are Your Chances for Slimming Down?

I know that many teen-agers feel, no matter how hard they try, that nothing ever works, that they're doomed to be fat. Adults, too, often feel that adolescence is the worst time in a lifetime to try to lose weight, and it probably is. That's because your body is geared to growth right now and it seems to be working against your efforts to get yourself in good shape.

I'm not going to tell you it's easy at your age, but I am going to tell you it can be done. I know; I've helped many of my patients slim down very successfully without making their lives miserable. If you honestly want to lose weight enough to make a real try, then you can do it.

Some teen-agers will always find it harder to be thin than others and that usually depends on past history. Some of you were born fat and stayed fat up until this moment, while some of you started off thin and gradually gained too much weight.

The first group is going to have a harder time losing. Unfortunately if you were overweight as a baby and young child, you developed a much larger number of fat cells than somebody your age who's always been thin. These fat cells, which make up the fat tissue in your body, are always ready to store the fat supplied by any calories you take in which aren't burned up in activity.

Once you've got excess fat cells, you can't get rid of them, *but* you can always shrink them down to a smaller size by not overfeeding them.

Some people also have a tough time getting and staying

thin because a tendency toward overweight can be inherited. Statistically, if one or both of your parents are fat, the chances are higher that you'll be overweight too. Perhaps you've inherited a body build that encourages fat storage, or maybe you were born with excess fat cells. Then you will have to fight harder than those long, lanky, lucky people who can eat from now until next month without gaining weight. I remember a boy, a friend of my teen-age son, whom we all envied. He was very tall, very thin, with long legs and arms. He used to eat us all under the table and never gained an ounce. Our family was not that lucky. We had to be more careful.

The body is made up of fat tissue and "lean body mass" (which means everything but the fat and includes all your bones, muscles, etc.). When we talk about overweight, we are simply saying that your body contains too high a percentage of fat tissue in relation to your lean body mass. What we have to do is get rid of some of it, leaving you with a higher percentage of other tissue. The way we do it is to shrink the fat cells you already have, and prevent you from *continuing* to develop a superabundance of them—which you will do if you stay fat.

Could It Be Glands?

Overweight teen-agers always ask me whether their problem could be "glands." Not too many years ago, a "sluggish" thyroid gland was considered the culprit in any case of superfat. The theory was very handy because then a fat person could simply pop pills and shed pounds with no effort at all.

Well, I'm sorry to have to tell you that in 999 cases out of 1,000, your problem isn't "glands." If you are very fat *and* very short, though, you might be the exception, and I suggest you have your doctor check out the possibility by making the proper tests.

It is simply not true that overweight people start off, in the vast majority of cases, with a low metabolism rate, though here's the kicker that makes the idea so popular— once a person *is* fat, she exercises less, slowing down her metabolism (the rate at which she burns up calories).

Taking thyroid pills without good reason is dangerous (it can affect your heart) and useless as well. You will lose weight while you're taking the pills, but you'll gain it right back when you stop, perhaps with a few extra pounds thrown in because the pills depress the thyroid gland's own functioning for a while even after you stop taking them. Furthermore, you will not have lost much fat tissue, but rather lean body mass, calcium and nitrogen—which is not what we're after.

And Other Pills?

Taking *any* pills for the purpose, of reducing, unless your doctor has found a *real* medical need for them, is a bad idea. Appetite suppressants won't work, they're habit-forming, and they're dangerous. And so are injections. Stay away from them.

"I Want to Lose a Lot of Weight Fast."

I can't blame you for wanting to get thin in a hurry but I'm not going to recommend it, for three reasons.

1. Losing weight too rapidly can actually stunt your growth. This is a medical fact. If you lose pounds fast before you have finished growing, you may end up a lot shorter than you would have otherwise. The reason is this: you are

still in a growing period. If you lose weight too fast by taking in too few calories, your body will start burning up its protein in order to furnish enough energy to keep going. This is called negative nitrogen balance. If a growing person remains in negative nitrogen balance for any period of time beyond a few days, this will slow down or stop growth. This loss of growth, furthermore, can't be made up later on.

2. Crash diets, the crazy restrictive diets many people go on, allow you to lose a lot of weight in the first week or two *but* that is due almost entirely to a loss of *water* and not fat tissue. Once you go off the diet, you accumulate the normal amount of water again and you're right back where you started. You've suffered for nothing and you feel more hopeless than ever. I'm sure you've tried it and you know what I'm talking about.

3. No one can stay on a weird and/or unsatisfying diet for very long. So what will happen is that you'll lose some weight, go off the diet, gain the weight back. You could spend the rest of your life losing and gaining weight, and that is not healthy. Better to stay steadily fat than turn into a yo-yo.

What I'd like to help you do is permanently reduce your weight, slowly and steadily, so that it will stay lost. Because you are still growing, you don't have to lose as much as you think in actual pounds. Usually, unless you are excessively heavy, that means merely *not* gaining. Then, as you grow, your weight will catch up with your height.

If you are much too heavy, then a slow gradual loss, perhaps a pound a week, is enough. That doesn't sound like much, but do you know that adds up to fifty-two pounds in a year? In actuality, it's even more than that because you're growing at the same time.

"I Don't Know Why I'm Fat."

Weight involves just two factors—how many calories you take in each day and how many calories you use up. If at the end of the day you've taken in *more* calories than you've used up, you'll gain weight. If, at the end of the day you've taken in the *same* number of calories you've used up, you'll stay the same. And if you've taken in *fewer* calories than you've used up, you'll lose weight. It's that simple.

We all use·up a certain number of calories just by living and breathing. This is called basal metabolism, the amount used to keep the body going at rest. This amount varies very little from person to person.

The rest of the calories are burned up by physical activity. Exercise. A dirty word? It is to most overweight people. Studies have shown that, while many overweight youngsters may eat even less than their thin friends, they also do much less exercise, perhaps only a third as much. And other research shows that when regular exercise is added to the daily regime, weight loss can be dramatic and permanent.

Though you probably don't want to think about it, I'm sure you know what I'm talking about. Do you ride a bicycle, walk a lot every day, climb stairs instead of taking elevators, really participate in gym class? Or do you sit in one spot as much as you can? At the same time, are you eating like a typical teen-ager? I know that adolescents have tremendous appetites. Because you're growing so fast now, you do need more food than you did before. But if you concentrate on sweets and starches, snacks and nibbles, you're consuming vast numbers of calories. And, if you spend most of your time on your fanny instead of your feet, you're not going to burn them up.

And you'll be fat.

Here's My Solution

Losing weight is very simple. You can cut down on the number of calories you eat. Or increase the number of calories you burn up. Or you can do both.

Let me give you an example. We'll suppose you want to lose a pound a week, four pounds in a month, fifty-two pounds in a year. A pound of fat equals about 3,500 calories. That means, in order to lose a pound of fat, you have to get rid of 3,500 calories each week.

That's 500 calories a day. You could do that by continuing to get the same amount of exercise you always have, and cutting down your food by 500 calories. Or you could eat the same, and burn up an extra 500 calories in exercise.

Or you could cut down on your food by only 250 calories and increase your exercise by only 250 calories.

That's really a very minor change when you consider that switching from three glasses (about 160 calories per glass) of regular whole milk a day to three glasses of skimmed milk (about 80 calories per glass) will save almost the entire 250 calories. Refraining from devouring three fudge cookies or two orange sodas will do the same.

To get rid of 250 calories, you need only bike ride for half an hour or swim for about twenty minutes. Brisk walking will do it in about forty minutes. See page 48 for a list of kinds of exercise with their caloric equivalents.

Most people your age, those who aren't extremely overweight, don't need to lose even as much as a pound a week, and could thin down nicely by cutting out only 100 calories in food and adding 100 in exercise a day (a chocolate cupcake and a moderate walk).

"I Thought You Said No Calorie Counting."

I did and I mean it, though you do have to have some idea of what your food and your activity are worth in order to understand what you're doing. If you follow my suggestions, coming later in this chapter, you'll be cutting calories without noticing them.

Rather than counting up the calories of everything you eat, which is a bore and which most people tend to forget about after a little while, try keeping a *diary* of what you eat. Write down every single bit of food that passes your lips, along with every small amount of exercise you get each day, and you'll soon see what it is that's making you fat or thin. Seeing these things written down makes it impossible not to be aware of what is *really* happening.

Your Parents' Role

I've told your parents in the last chapter that they can't make you lose weight, they can't force you to eat the right foods and they can't force you to exercise. It's all up to you. If you want to get thin badly enough right now, you'll manage to do it. If you don't, it's your decision. Maybe you'll want to wait until you're more mature. Some teen-agers, in truth, find it much too hard to tackle weight at a time when growing up is all they can handle, and they should relax, forget about it, and work on the problem later when they've stopped growing. I think I've made it very clear that your parents shouldn't nag, pester, scold, embarrass, check up, or bug you about your weight, but that they should be available for discussion if you want it.

I've asked your parents to do a couple of things before they cut out.

First, to be sure there's a good accurate scale in the house on which you can weigh in (alone) once a week.

Then, I've suggested that they help you in any way they can, short of bugging you, to get more exercise.

I've asked them to take you to your doctor for a complete checkup.

And I've asked them to fatproof the house. That's important. It means getting rid of all the junk food, the stuff with lots of calories and no (or very little) nourishment. Examples: potato chips, cheese spreads, cake, sodas, cookies, candy. I've told them to clear the house of all of it, so it won't be there to tempt you. No matter if you have a skinny brother and a thin father, the junk food is disappearing and it won't be available for anyone. Because it's unrealistic to expect one member of the household—you—to resist a certain food if it's around, everyone in the family will have to eat the same way.

I've explained that there must be a good supply of fresh fruits and vegetables and hard cheese in the house.

That the only liquids to be there are skimmed milk, low-calorie sodas, fruit juices, and water.

That there's to be no calorie counting or measuring of portions, and you're to be allowed to eat as much as you want. It's important that you don't go hungry or unsatisfied or feel deprived. If, after a moderate first portion at mealtimes, you want more, by all means have it—except for the starches.

That rich desserts have to go, except on very special occasions. The only allowed desserts are fresh fruit, hard cheese or diet gelatin.

That, whenever possible, everyone in the family should eat together, especially dinner. That it's important for everyone to eat three *real* meals, meals that are well-balanced and nutritious, rather than an endless round of snacks. And that meals should be leisurely and relaxed.

Your Role

Your part in all this is to try to accept the fact that fat foods won't be around the house, so you won't get them at home. And to try to refrain as much as you can from forays into the outside world for them.

You'll end up, just by doing this one thing, with a well-balanced nutritive diet that's healthy and satisfying, and one you can continue to eat all your life without "suffering." You'll lose weight and you'll keep it off. I promise you.

You will probably complain, as my teen-agers do: "There's nothing decent to eat in the house"; "I'm going to starve to death if you keep this up." And you're probably never going to think carrots or pears are as good as french fries and butterscotch pudding. But you'll be amazed at how good the carrots and pears (and apples and cheese and chicken and even broccoli) are going to taste when you're really hungry and there's nothing else around. Keep in mind that these are the foods that will keep you healthy as well as thin—and you need them every day. Many vitamins and minerals can't be stored by the body and have to be replaced daily.

Because you're going to be eating a real breakfast, instead of your former cookie or maybe nothing at all, you won't be so ravenous in the morning that you'll need to patronize the candy machine at school and, besides, you may even find an improvement in your report card.

Because you'll be having a proper lunch and a leisurely satisfying dinner, with all the food you can eat, you may not want to continue your steady trek back and forth to the kitchen for snacks, all evening long. But, if you do, you'll find only healthy snacks, non-fattening. Most overweight people do a lot of their low-quality eating at night just before they go to bed when it won't be burned off in activity.

Remember, there's no need to cut down on the amount of food you eat. Your big appetite is normal and you should eat all you want so you won't end up feeling deprived and unsatisfied.

"OK, I'll Go Out and Eat What I Want."

I don't expect you to stick religiously to a certain diet, and I feel it's unrealistic to expect that you'll never touch another bag of potato chips or never go out with your friends for pizza and Coke. The big difference in your life will be that you won't get instant gratification at home. And you won't be too likely to feel like getting dressed at 9:30 at night to go out and buy doughnuts. Chances are you'll make do with skimmed milk and cheese and fruit.

Because small changes in calorie intake are all most teen-agers need, eliminating the binges at home where you do most of your eating could be all that's necessary. If it doesn't turn out that way, then you must try to eliminate the binges outside the house as much as you can. If your job is to cut down the fat tissue you're carrying around, then you have to try to pass up the goodies or have a little less than you used to. Have a hamburger and forget the french fries. Eat the pizza but substitute a low-calorie soda for the Coke. If your friends are truly that, they'll respect your feelings and self-control. Even if you do eat the wrong foods now and then, it won't matter too much if you don't overdo it. Don't feel guilty—just recognize you're doing it.

But *don't bring the stuff home!* Not too long ago, I explained my non-diet to a very fat teen-age boy and his parents. When he came to my office a few months later, he hadn't lost a pound. Instead he'd gained five. He told me

he'd followed my suggestions, his mother refused to stock in
junk foods, and he'd even cut down a little on his outside
binges.

I couldn't understand it. Everyone was doing his part and
the boy gained five pounds. Maybe, I thought, he was one of
the rare few with a glandular problem though I'd found no
evidence of it after a thorough examination. Then, a couple
of weeks later I received a call from his mother. Cleaning
out his room, she'd found hidden deep in a closet a supply of
Milky Ways big enough to feed fifteen fat teen-agers for a
year.

When she confronted her son with the evidence, he
became very indignant about his invasion of privacy. Then
he said, "Dr. Eden never told me not to have a little snack in
my room when I needed it."

In fact, I hadn't. I'd never thought of it.

If you really want to lose the fat that makes you so
unhappy, you're not going to look for exceptions to the
rules I've outlined. What you do outside is one thing,
though a little moderation is only reasonable, but in the
house there can be no exceptions.

The Rest of the Rules

Aside from the no-junk-food-in-the-house prohibition, here
are the rest of the rules:

No fluids except:
   Skimmed milk
   Low-calorie sodas
   Water and tea
   Fruit juices
No desserts except:
   A piece of raw fruit
   Hard cheese

Low-calorie gelatin
No bread except:
 1 thin slice for breakfast
 2 thin slices for school-lunch sandwiches

Other than that, there are no restrictions except that I suggest you use polyunsaturated margarine, eat only three or four eggs a week, eat more (non-shell) fish and poultry, and take one multivitamin each day.

What's going to come of all this, if you stick with it, is a change in your eating habits. Gradually you'll learn to like the more nutritious foods because the others won't be around. When you're hungry, you're not going to be too choosey—you may prefer a cream puff over all else, but if it's not there the next best thing could be an apple. I remember a camp hike I went on when I was a kid. We miscalculated our distance and by the time we reached our campsite, it was getting dark. The only food we had along to eat that didn't require building a fire and cooking was a few cans of sardines. I'd never liked sardines before, but I was hungry and I ate them and thought they were the most delicious things I'd ever tasted. I still love sardines today.

Gradually you'll find your craving for sweets and starches will diminish to the point where you can easily handle it. No, it won't disappear, but you'll have found substitutes for the junk that will satisfy you most of the time.

You'll learn to concentrate your eating at meals instead of spreading your food out over the entire day, giving yourself time to burn up calories.

The Ideal Foods for Teens

In broad terms, let me outline an ideal diet for you.

Breakfast: Tomato juice (lower in calories than other

juices), an egg with bacon or ham. One slice of toast. Glass of skimmed milk. A non-egg day could include juice, cereal (preferably whole grain), fruit and skimmed milk. Or perhaps toast with American cheese.

Lunch: If you buy your lunch at school, it's sure to be full of starch and sugar and low in protein. But, if that's all that is available, eat it. If you take lunch from home, you'll probably feel you have to take a sandwich. Use thin-sliced bread and some form of protein filling, such as tuna fish or chicken. A piece of raw fruit. Fruit juice or small container of skimmed milk or a diet soda.

After-school snack: Skimmed milk. Fruit.

Dinner: Salad, meat or fish, vegetables, potatoes, fruit. Beverages with meals: Skimmed milk, juice, diet soda, water.

I've explained to your parents the dangers of serving you too much food that promotes the accumulation of cholesterol in the blood, such as red meat, eggs, and whole milk. And I've mentioned that it's a good idea to cut down on the amount of salt used in cooking. Excessive cholesterol may eventually lead to heart attacks. Too much salt may lead to high blood pressure. Try not to use extra at the table.

If you are eating well-balanced meals, you won't need extra vitamins. However, because many teen-agers skip certain kinds of vegetables and fruits, a multivitamin a day is a good idea. And a balanced diet will help you reach your full height. As Dr. Jean Mayer, the Harvard nutritionist, points out, "Everyone needs a balanced diet, but teen-agers need it even more than older people. If they are short-changed on any of the basic food elements, they may fail to reach their full heights, thereby making themselves more stocky and dumpy than they need to be."

Weighing In

I don't believe in weighing oneself every day. Once a week is enough. Because your goal is a gradual reduction of weight or slowing down of gain, you shouldn't think in terms of a day or even a week, but months.

Helpful Hints on the Subject of Food

• Do all your eating *sitting down* at the dining room table. Never eat in the kitchen or in your room. Never eat in front of the TV set—that's where most people take in the most calories, it has been found. Snacks included.

• Chew every bite slowly. Take your time. Wait between bites. Wait between courses. Psychologists of the behavior modification school have uncovered the fact that eating slowly is more satisfying; that, for example, there is less desire for a rich dessert after a slowly consumed meal than there is after a meal that's been bolted down.

• Get most of your calories at mealtimes.

• Don't do anything else while you're eating—don't watch television, read a book, talk on the phone, or play games. Conversation is fine, though.

• Keep a record for a week of what you've eaten, every bite, before you begin my non-diet—I'm sure you're eating much more of the wrong foods than you realize. Notice your moods when you feel especially hungry. Are you eating because you're actually hungry, or because you're depressed or bored?

• If you see that you eat to overcome depression or restlessness or boredom, do something instead—go for a walk, call a friend, wash your hair, read a book.

• Get together with friends who also need to lose

weight, perhaps have weekly meetings. This can bolster your willpower and make it more fun. Or get your doctor to monitor you.

• Drink a big glass of ice water or low-calorie soda when hunger overwhelms you.

• Always leave some food on your plate.

• Never skip a meal.

• If you absolutely must eat a high-calorie food, eat only half the amount you formerly did.

Stand, Walk, Run, Jump

And now we'll have to discuss that unpopular subject (at least among most overweight teen-agers)—exercise.

As I've discussed, scientific research has shown that perhaps the most important reason adolescents are overweight is that they get so little exercise. Think about yourself. Do you actually move your muscles to any appreciable degree every day? Do you run, or even walk fast; do you play any games; do you do exercises regularly; do you ride a bike or climb a lot of stairs? If you're honest, I think you'll find you don't do too much, and that your favorite position is slumped in a comfortable chair.

If you realize that almost every calorie you eat is busily turning to fat unless you burn it up in activity, maybe you'll see how important exercise is. In fact, it's been shown that weight is lost more quickly and efficiently when diet *and* exercise are combined. Dieting will take off pounds, of course, but it will have to be much more stringent than if you exercise too. An added bonus is that not only does exercise speed up the process of burning up calories, but it speeds up your metabolism even after you're finished and are lying flat on your back.

You don't have to exercise for hours and hours at a time

to lose weight, as most youngsters think. Biking for a half hour a day, for example, will take care of 1,750 calories a week. An hour a day of good hard exercise will take off at least a pound in a week. And if you're following my non-diet, think what the combination will do.

Exercising every single day is very important, much better than violent activity once in a while. It will help you lose weight and it will firm up the flab at the same time, along with toning up your heart and lungs. I can't tell you exactly what kind of exercise to get, because everyone's tastes are different, but I will say that sports and games are a far better way to get it than sitting-up exercises. Not because the exercises don't work—they do—but because you're not too likely to stick with them.

Take advantage of all the opportunities you get—walk to school instead of taking a bus or begging your mother for a ride, walk up stairs instead of taking elevators, take your bike to the store, surprise your parents (and yourself) by raking the lawn or weeding the garden, really participate in gym class. In other words, do anything you can that moves your muscles. One advantage you have, being overweight, is that you'll burn up more calories than a thin person doing the very same thing.

Exercise won't make you hungry either—that idea has been proved to be a myth.

Keep in mind that exercise that uses a lot of muscles, like running or brisk walking, will burn more energy than exercise that uses only a specific few, like driving golf balls or doing push-ups. And the more vigorously you pursue it, the more calories you consume. For example, walking four miles an hour will use up about twice as many calories in the same length of time as walking two miles an hour. Jogging will use more; and running the most.

Don't despair. As you get thinner, you'll *feel* more like getting around. As you get around, you'll get thinner.

Are You with Me?

If you've stayed with me right up to this point, then I think half your battle is won. Obviously, you honestly want to be thin. And, if you do, you'll manage it.

14

The Last Word

Hopefully, I've convinced you that your children will be healthier as well as happier if they grow up thin. Hopefully, I've helped you discover how to help them do it.

"Fatproofing" your children against becoming overweight adults, lowering their risk of ever being fat, is one of a parent's most important jobs. We've found out how dangerous it is to be fat. We've discovered in only the last few years that most fat adults learned how to be fat when they were children. We know that overweight adults, though they may manage to lose weight, usually have to keep doing it over and over again.

And we know now that the only sure way to prevent the inevitable psychological, physical and social problems of overweight that can blight your children's lives is never to let them get fat in the first place. The next best thing is to start slimming them down *now*, before another day goes by.

I'm not recommending a nation of parents who won't let their children near a piece of candy or within smelling distance of a chocolate cupcake. I'm not recommending rigidity, the counting of calories, the weighing of hamburger patties; nor do I propose that parents spend all their time monitoring what their children put in their mouths and ordering them to run around the block.

But I do propose feeding babies a nutritionally well-balanced diet so that they gain weight at a steady but unmeteoric rate; teaching toddlers to eat only a proper amount of food and to like the food that's good for them, and *not* teaching them that food solves all problems and brings love; helping school-age and adolescent children avoid the junk foods that have unfortunately become part of our culture; encouraging them all to get exercise and to eat the healthy foods that will keep them (or help them become) slender and happy.

It's not hard. It's not complicated. It's safe and medically sound. And it works.

It's guilt-free. When you refuse to stuff your children full of too much of the wrong foods, you're not depriving them of love. You're only depriving them of fat and plenty of problems.

The goal is to grow up thin and *stay* thin. Remember, if your children are fat *now*, they'll probably be fat *later*. If they're thin now, they'll undoubtedly stay thin forever.

Start fatproofing now. The earlier you begin, the better your children's chances of growing up thin.

APPENDIX I

*Caloric Counts of Some High-Calorie Snack Foods**

Item	Calories
Fritos corn chips (1 ounce)	166
Wise potato chips (1 ounce)	162
Hunt's Snack Pack canned butterscotch pudding ($\frac{1}{2}$ cup)	238
Cool 'n Creamy Dark frozen chocolate pudding ($\frac{1}{2}$ cup)	203
Pepperidge Farm lemon turnover	341
Morton honey bun	170
Drake's Devil Dog ($2\frac{1}{4}$ ounces)	307
Drake's Ring Ding ($2\frac{1}{2}$ ounces)	366
Hostess chocolate-topped cupcakes ($1\frac{1}{2}$ ounces)	145
Hostess fried apple pie (4 ounces)	363
Thomas' corn muffin	180
Hawaiian Punch Very Berry (8 ounces)	110
Welchade grapeade (8 ounces)	120
Hi-C Cherry Drink (8 ounces)	122
Keebler Old Fashioned chocolate chip cookies (1)	79
Nabisco peanut creme Fancy Patties (1)	198
Pepperidge Farm Lido sandwich cookie (1)	91
Yum Yums coconut caramel cookies (1)	83
Nestle's butterscotch morsels (1 ounce)	150
Hershey chocolate chips (1 ounce)	152

* Excerpted from *The Brand-Name Calorie Counter* by Corinne Netzer with Elaine Chaback, preface by Irwin M. Stillman, M.D. Copyright © 1969, 1971, 1972 by Corinne T. Netzer. Used with permission of Dell Publishing Co., Inc.

M & Ms candy-coated chocolate (1 ounce)   130
Nabisco Thin Mint   122
Nabisco chocolate-covered nuts (1 ounce)   159
Oreo cookies (1)   50
Keebler's vanilla cream sandwich cookies (1)   85
Nabisco Twirls chocolate-covered marshmallow (1)   133
Keebler's pecan fudge brownies (1)   260
Kellogg's Pop-Tarts (1.8 ounces)   207
Thomas' date nut bread (1 slice)   100
Kellogg's Sugar Frosted Flakes (1 cup)   143
Quaker Cap'n Crunch (1 cup)   163
Nabisco Rice Honeys (1 cup)   151
Downyflake frozen french toast (1 slice)   138
Borden's cherry-vanilla milk shake (8 ounces)   291
Nestle's Quik Shake (chocolate malted, 8 ounces)   263
Buitoni Instant frozen pizza (2¾ ounces)   139
Banquet Fried Chicken frozen dinner (11 ounces)   542
Gebhardt Instant canned chili con carne (1 cup)   478
Franco-American canned spaghetti and meatballs
    (1 cup)   260
Shak-A-Pudd'n chocolate pudding (½ cup)   200
Pepsi-Cola (8 ounces)   104
Crush grape soda   126

APPENDIX II

*Calorie Counts of Some Common Foods**

Breads and Cereals

Rye bread, regular slice	70
thin slice	55
White bread, regular slice	75
thin slice	60
Whole-wheat bread, regular slice	70
thin slice	55
Bran muffin, 2¾ inches	130
Corn muffin, 2¾ inches	150
English muffin, 3½ inches	135
Hamburger or frankfurter roll	120
Graham crackers, 4 small or 2 medium	55
Saltines, 2	35
Plain doughnut	125
Pancake, 4-inch	60
Pizza, plain cheese, 5½-inch slice	185
Waffle, 1 average-size	210
Puffed corn cereal, presweetened, 1 cup	115
Corn flakes, 1 cup	95
Farina, 1 cup cooked	105
Oatmeal, cooked, 1 cup	130
Puffed rice, 1 cup	60
Macaroni, cooked, plain, ¾ cup	115

* From "Calories and Weight," U.S. Department of Agriculture, 1972.

Macaroni with cheese, ¾ cup	360
Noodles, cooked, ¾ cup	150
Rice, cooked, ¾ cup	140
Spaghetti in tomato sauce with cheese, ¾ cup	195
Spaghetti with meat balls, ¾ cup	250

Meats

Hamburger, broiled, regular ground beef, 3 ounces	245
Hamburger, broiled, lean ground round, 3 ounces	185
Corned beef hash, ½ cup	155
Roast beef, lean only, 3 ounces	140 –205
Pot roast, lean only, 3 ounces	165
Steak, broiled, lean only, 3 ounces	175
Lamb chop or roast leg, lean only, 3 ounces	160
Bacon, 2 thin slices	60
Pork chop, lean only, 3 ounces	230
Bologna, 2 ounces	170
Pork sausage, 2 ounces	270
Frankfurter, 1 ounce	155
Boiled ham, 2 ounces	135
Chicken, broiled, ¼ small broiler	185
Chicken, fried, 1 whole leg	225
Turkey, roasted, 3 ounces	150 –175

Fish

Bluefish, baked, 3 ounces	135
Salmon, broiled, 3 ounces	155
Tuna, packed in oil, drained, 3 ounces	170

Eggs

Fried in fat, 1 large	100
Hard- or soft-cooked, 1 large or poached	80
Scrambled in fat, 1 large plus milk	110

Nuts

Cashews, 5 large	60
Peanuts, 2 tablespoons	105

Milk and Milk Products

Skimmed milk, fresh or reconstituted dry, 1 cup	90
Whole milk, 1 cup	160
Heavy cream, 1 tablespoon	55
Sour cream, 1 tablespoon	30
1 cup	505
Yogurt, from partially skimmed milk, 1 cup	120
Chocolate milk, 1 cup	210
Chocolate milkshake, 12 ounces	520
Cocoa, all milk, 1 cup	235
Ice cream, plain, ½ cup	145
Ice milk, hard-serve, ½ cup	110
soft-serve, 1 cup	130
Fruit sherbet, ½ cup	130
American process cheese, 1 ounce	105
Cheddar, natural, 1 ounce	115
Cottage cheese, creamed, 2 tablespoons	30
Cream cheese, 2 tablespoons	105
Swiss cheese, 1 ounce	105

Other Beverages

Cola, 8 ounces	95
Root beer, 8 ounces	100
Fruit flavors, carbonated, 8 ounces	115

Soups

Bouillon, 1 cup	30
Chicken noodle, 1 cup	60

Cream of mushroom, 1 cup   135
Split pea, 1 cup   145
Tomato, prepared with water, 1 cup   90
    prepared with milk, 1 cup   170

Vegetables

Cole slaw, with mayonnaise-type dressing, ½ cup   60
Carrots, ½ cup   20
Celery, 2 8-inch stalks   10
Cucumber, pared, ¾-inch slice   5
Tomatoes, 1 medium   35
Green lima beans, ½ cup   90
Green beans, ½ cup   15
Broccoli, ½ cup flower stalks   20
Corn on cob or ½ cup kernels   70
Peas, ½ cup   60
Potatoes, baked, 5 ounces   90
Potatoes, french fried, 10 2-inch pieces   155
Potatoes, hash browned, ½ cup   225
Spinach, ½ cup   20
Sweet potatoes, 6 ounces   155

Fruit

Apples, 2½ inches   70
Bananas, 1 6-inch   80
Berries, ½ cup   30–50
Cantaloupe, half of 5-inch size   50–60
Oranges, 3-inch   75
Peaches, 2 inches   35
Pineapple, ½ cup diced   40
Raisins, ½ cup   230
Watermelon, 2-pound wedge   115
Fruit canned in heavy syrup, ½ cup   100
Prunes, sweetened, cooked, ½ cup   250

Juices

Tomato juice, ½ cup	20
Grapefruit, unsweetened, ½ cup	50
Grape, ½ cup	80
Orange, ½ cup	55
Prune, ½ cup	100

Fats and Oils

Butter or margarine, 1 pat	50
Peanut butter, 1 tablespoon	95
Salad oil, 1 tablespoon	125

Desserts and Sweets

Angelcake, 2-inch piece	105
Chocolate cake, chocolate icing, 2 inches	345
Gingerbread, 2-inch square	170
Sponge cake, 2-inch sector	135
Yellow cake, 2-inch sector	205
Caramels, 3 medium	115
Fudge, plain, 1 ounce	120
Jellybeans, 10	105
Marshmallows, 4 large	90
Milk chocolate, 1-ounce bar	150
Chocolate syrup, 1 tablespoon	50
Jam, jelly, 1 tablespoon	55
Honey, 1 tablespoon	65
Syrup, 1 tablespoon	55
Cookies, 3-inch	120
Apple pie, portion	300
Coconut custard pie	270
Pecan pie	430
Custard, baked, ½ cup	140
Gelatin, plain, ½ cup	70
Bread pudding with raisins, ½ cup	250

"Extras"

Hamburger with roll, 2-ounce patty	265
Hot dog with roll	245
Pizza, plain cheese, $5\frac{1}{2}$-inch slice	185
Popcorn, oil and salt, 1 cup	40
Potato chips, 10 medium	115

Index

absorption, food, 22
accidents, overweight and incidence of, 6, 13, 15–16
adipose cells, development of, 24–25
  age factor, 26
  excess, management of, 27–28
adolescents, weight gain and loss, 3
  adipose cell growth, 169
  calorie counting, 195
  diet rules, 199–200, 202–203
  diets, 170–171, 200–201
  exercise, 183–185, 193, 194, 203–204
  mealtimes, 180–183
  medications, 170, 191
  outside eating, 179–180, 198–199
  parent role, 165–168, 177–179, 195–196
  physician role, 175
  rapid vs. gradual loss, 191–192
  reasons for overweight, 190–191
  slimming down, 189–190
  snacking, 197–198
  social and psychological aspects, 17, 118, 172–175, 187–189
  thinning tips, 176–177
  weighing in, 202
advancement, job, overweight and, 19
advertising, eating habits and, 31

age
  adipose cell development, 25, 26
  fatness risk, 65–69
  See also adolescents; babies; one-year olds; preschoolers; school-age children
Allon, Natalie, 18
American Academy of Pediatrics, 77
American Public Health Association, 60
appetite
  in babies, 35–36
  decrease in, 100–101
  eating habits and, 32–33
  exercise and, 50
  genetic factors of, 22
  vs. hunger, 33–36
  in preschoolers, 119–121, 132–133
appetite suppressants. See medications
arthritis, overweight and incidence of, 13, 15
atherosclerosis, overweight and incidence of, 14

babies, feeding, 2
  amounts and schedule, 76–79
  appetite, 93–94
  attitude, mother's, 94–95
  breast vs. bottle feeding, 79–81, 85
  burping, 83